Classic Storybook Cross-stitch

Classic Storybook Cross-stitch

Gillian Souter

LITTLE, BROWN AND COMPANY
Boston New York London

A LITTLE, BROWN BOOK

First published in Great Britain in 2000
by Little, Brown and Company (UK)

Created and designed by Off the Shelf Publishing,
32 Thomas Street, Lewisham, NSW 2049, Australia

Copyright © Off the Shelf Publishing, 2000
The moral right of the author has been asserted.

A CIP catalogue record for this book
is available from the British Library

ISBN 0-316-85401-8

10 9 8 7 6 5 4 3 2 1

Produced by Phoenix Offset
Printed and bound in China

Little, Brown and Company (UK)
Brettenham House
Lancaster Place
London WC2E 7EN

Contents

Introduction

I can think of few undertakings more pleasant than to design a range of cross-stitch projects based on much-loved children's book characters. That's perhaps the reason that this third collection is seeing the light: after writing Storybook Favourites in Cross-stitch and the second volume More Storybook Cross-stitch, I initially thought enough was enough! However, popular demand for more designs and the wealth of beautifully illustrated stories on my bookshelf have inspired this volume. It has a somewhat more traditional feel to it, drawing from such wonderful picture books as Guess How Much I Love You and the Old Bear series by Jane Hissey, which is why I've put the word 'classic' in the title. It is also something of a world tour of children's literature, with favourites such as Pinocchio from Italy, Frog from the Netherlands, America's Wizard of Oz, the Australian Gumnuts, the Little Prince from France, and the very British work of Beatrix Potter. Some favourite figures, such as Wally and Kipper, have crossed all boundaries. I'm sure you'll find plenty of inspiration here and that the suggested projects will please those children lucky enough to have you stitching for them!

Basic Techniques

Cross-stitch is one of the most popular of crafts and is extremely simple to learn. If you are new to this form of embroidery, this chapter will give you all the information you need to complete the projects in this book.

In cross-stitch, a pattern is transferred from a charted design to a piece of un-marked fabric. The chart is a grid of squares with symbols forming the design. A key tells you which colour of embroidery thread relates to which symbol on the chart. Working the design is simply a matter of stitching a series of crosses in the appropriate colour according to the arrangement on the chart.

Types of Fabric

Cross-stitch fabrics are evenly woven, that is, they have the same number of threads over a given distance both vertically and horizontally. Aida fabric, formed with bands of threads, is often used. There are many types of fabric woven in single threads: these can be made of various fibres but they're referred to in this book simply as linen.

The size of each stitch is determined by the number of fabric threads over which you sew and by the number of bands or threads per inch of fabric (known as the fabric count). Most fabric counts are still given in inches, even in countries which have adopted the metric system. Linen 26 has twenty-six threads per inch of fabric and

each stitch covers two threads (to prevent the embroidery thread gliding under a fabric thread) so there are thirteen stitches per inch. With Linen 30, there are fifteen stitches per inch: the larger the fabric count, the smaller the stitches will be.

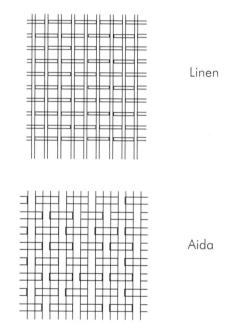

Linen

Aida

Estimating Size

The instructions for each project specify the type of fabric used to stitch it and the amount of fabric required. When you choose a fabric with a different thread count, you will need to calculate what the size of the stitched design will be. Use the following rule: finished size equals the design stitch count divided by the fabric thread count.

When using linen, you stitch over two threads. Therefore, a stitch count of 50 x 50 (i.e. 50 squares on the chart each way) must be divided by 13, if using Linen 26, or by 15 (Linen 30) and so on. Aida also comes in various counts. if using Aida 14, divide the stitch count by 14. Multiply the result by 2.5 to convert from inches into centimetres.

Colouring Fabric

Evenweave fabrics for cross-stitch are available in a wide range of colours, but unusual shades are often more expensive. If you can't find the shade you want, or if you have white or off-white fabric to spare, you could try tinting it yourself. Acrylic paint, when mixed with plenty of water to make a wash, can be brushed on to damp fabric. This will probably dry a slightly darker shade and can look a little blotchy, which looks fine as sky. Do not use this method for a project that will need washing. For a more even colouring and for permanence, use a fabric dye, following the instructions on the packet.

Preparing the Fabric

To prevent the fabric from fraying, zigzag the edges on a sewing machine or simply use masking tape which can later be removed.

Locate the centre of the fabric by folding it in half and then in half again. If you are working on a large design, mark the centre with a pin and use a coloured thread to tack from side to side and from top to bottom, each time tacking through the centre mark. This should quarter your fabric. When you start cross-stitching, make sure the centre of the design (indicated by arrows on the chart) matches the centre point of your fabric.

Embroidery Thread

All designs in this book have been stitched with DMC stranded cotton embroidery thread. If you wish to use a different brand, match the colours in the pictures as closely as possible or create your own combinations.

The key for each design lists: a symbol which appears in the chart, a corresponding DMC thread number, a colour name for easy identification, and the number of stitches to be made in that colour. It is impossible to gauge the exact amount of thread needed but this will give an idea of the relative quantities required for each colour. As a very rough guide, a block of 100 cross-stitches on Aida 14 requires 50 cm of embroidery thread using two strands at a time.

The six strands of the embroidery thread can be split into single strands, three lengths of double strands, or other combinations. The number of strands used depends on the count of your fabric. In general, using more strands will make your finished work more vivid, but if you use too many strands they will not fit neatly within the weave of the fabric. Below is a suggested number of strands for different fabric counts. It is a good idea, though, to add an extra strand when stitching the design on a dark fabric.

Count	Cross-stitch strands	Backstitch strands
Aida 11	3	2
Aida 14	2	1
Aida 18	2	1
Aida 22	1	1
Linen 16	3	2
Linen 20	2	1
Linen 28	2	1
Linen 32	1	1

Equipment

Use a blunt needle such as a small tapestry needle that will not split the fabric threads. Match the size of the needle to the size of the hole: a size 24 needle is suitable for Linen 20 or Aida 11 whereas a size 26 needle would be appropriate for Aida 14.

You will need two pairs of scissors: a small pair for trimming threads and a pair of shears for cutting the fabric.

If you are stitching a large design, or one that requires similar thread shades, your spare strands can easily become jumbled. To make a simple thread holder like the one pictured, cut a length of sturdy card and use a hole punch to cut holes at regular intervals. Mark the colour number and the appropriate symbol alongside the hole and tie threads as shown.

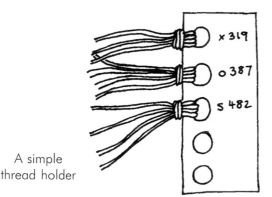

A simple thread holder

A frame or embroidery hoop will help you to stitch evenly and prevent warping, but it is not necessary for small designs. Choose a hoop which will fit the whole design, otherwise it may damage existing stitches.

Reading the Charts

Each square on the chart represents a full cross-stitch and each symbol represents a colour as specified in the key. A heavy line indicates where to backstitch and the key will tell you which colour to use for each section of backstitching. Arrows indicate the centre of the design.

Check the instructions regarding the position of the stitching on the fabric; if there are no specific instructions, orient the fabric to match the chart and stitch the design in the centre. Find the colour represented by the centre symbol and start on that block of colour.

Cut a 50 cm length of embroidery thread and gently split it into the appropriate number of strands. Let the strands dangle and untwist.

Cross-stitching

Thread the needle with the appropriate number of strands and bring it through the fabric, leaving 2 cm of waste thread at the back. Hold this tail carefully and make sure that your first four or five stitches secure it. Then trim any excess.

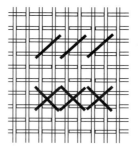

Forming cross-stitches on linen

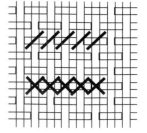

Forming cross-stitches on Aida

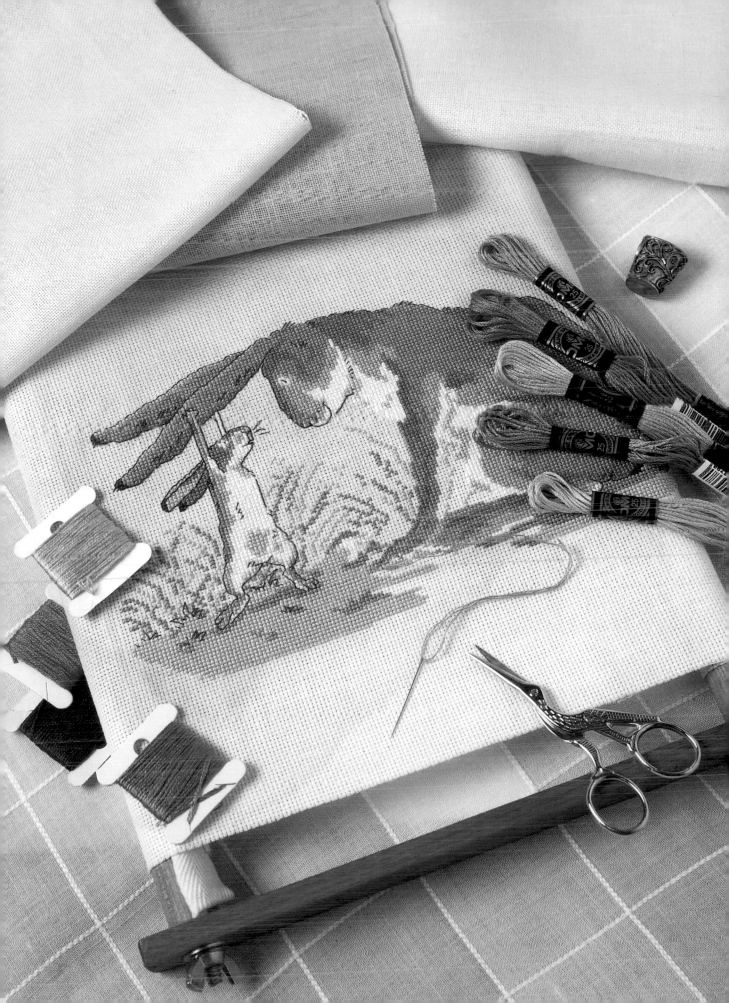

Stitch a series of diagonal bars running from left to right. Then, at the end of the row, return by stitching the top bars from right to left. Drop your needle to the bottom of the next row and repeat the process. Stitches in a sequence interlock, sharing holes with the neighbouring stitch.

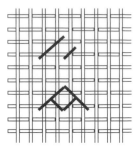

Forming two half-stitches

Remember, the number of threads crossed by a single stitch will depend on your fabric: on linen, each stitch covers two threads, on Aida each stitch covers one band of threads. This is shown more clearly in the two diagrams on page 10.

Always work horizontally rather than vertically and do not change directions; even though you may use more embroidery thread the result will look much neater.

Once you have stitched some crosses, use them as your reference point and count from them, rather than from the centre. Your tacked centre lines remain useful as a cross-check that you are counting correctly. Complete each block of colour, jumping short distances where necessary, but always securing the thread at the back by running the needle under existing threads. If blocks are some distance apart, finish off the first and start afresh.

To finish off each section, run your needle through the back of four or five stitches and trim the embroidery thread close to the cloth.

Half-stitch

Many of the charts contain some half-stitches or, as they are sometimes called, three-quarter stitches. These are indicated on the chart by a right-angled triangle and are usually found around the edges of a design. In this case, one diagonal of the cross-stitch is formed in the usual way, but the second stitch is brought down into the central hole of linen, or into the centre of an Aida block.

Where the chart indicates two half-stitches in the same square, you will need to decide which colour should predominate in the second diagonal.

Backstitch

Many of the charts include backstitching to define outlines and provide detail. It is indicated by a solid line on the chart. Back-stitch is always worked after cross-stitching is completed and is worked in a continuous line. The method is best described in the diagram below.

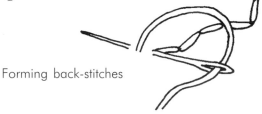

Forming back-stitches

Some Tips

It is important to keep your work as clean and fresh as possible. Don't leave unfinished work in an embroidery hoop for too long. When not in use, always secure the needle at the edge of the fabric to prevent rust marks or thread distortion.

Do not fold work-in-progress; roll it in a layer of tissue paper. A sheet of acetate (available from art supply shops) offers good protection for a large project.

Cut your embroidery thread, as you need it, into 50 cm lengths. Longer strands will start to fray towards the end.

If you are working a design with two strands here is a useful tip: cut a long single strand, thread both ends through the needle and catch the end loop at the back on your first stitch to neatly secure the end.

As you stitch, the thread tends to twist. This may produce uneven stitches so, if it happens, let the needle dangle from the fabric so that the thread can unwind.

When moving from one area of a colour to another patch of the same colour, don't jump the thread across the back if the gap will remain bare. Such leaps will show through the fabric in the finished work.

If you make an error in counting, do not try to rescue the embroidery thread for reuse. Use a pair of small pointed scissors to snip misplaced stitches and carefully pull out the strands, then stitch correctly with a new piece of embroidery thread.

Avoid the temptation to start or finish off with a knot; it will form a lump when the work is laid flat.

Teaching Children

Cross-stitch is an ideal introduction to needlecraft and the designs in this book may well tempt many boys and girls to take up the craft of cross-stitch and it is important to start them on simple and achievable projects which will not dampen their enthusiasm and deter their interest.

Here are some tips:

- Encourage children to practise the basic cross-stitch by creating coloured patterns on scrap fabric before tackling a design.

- Explain how the key works, making sure they understand that each symbol represents a particular colour.

- Children may like to colour in the key and the chart (you may photocopy a design from the book provided it is for personal use only).

- Choose a large count Aida fabric and a large blunt needle for them to work with.

- Choose a small design which has big blocks of solid colour. Introduce half-stitches only once they have mastered the full cross-stitch.

- Supervise backstitching to begin with. It may be appropriate for you to work the backstitch for younger children.

- Help children make their stitched design into a finished project that they can use or display.

- Help children to chart their own initials, name, or age, using the alphabet and number charts on pages 124-5. If they stitch their name and age on a design, it both personalises it and becomes a milestone in a child's life.

- Suggest that novices start with one of the simple designs charted on pages 122-3. These are in colour, so the stitcher doesn't need to refer to a key of symbols.

Nursery Days

The nicest way to welcome a baby is with a gift that will be cherished long into childhood. Here are some ideas that are certain to stand the test of time: the classic works of Beatrix Potter and May Gibbs as well as some heart-winning images from Guess How Much I Love You. All of them will bring charm to the nursery and perhaps even draw a smile from baby.

Jemima Puddle-Duck

Apart from Peter Rabbit, perhaps the most popular character that Beatrix Potter created is Jemima Puddle-Duck, a foolish but endearing farm duck who simply wants to raise her own ducklings. She first appeared in a minor role in The Tale of Tom Kitten and then featured in her own book, published in 1908. In The Tale of Jemima Puddle-Duck, the fond would-be-mother is beguiled by a handsome 'foxy gentleman' into laying her eggs in his woodshed and then stuffing herself with herbs in preparation for a dinner party. Jemima was a real

duck who lived at Hill Top Farm and much of the tale's great appeal comes from its delightful portrayal of farm life. This chapter also draws on the charming images of The Tale of Peter Rabbit and The Tale of Two Bad Mice.

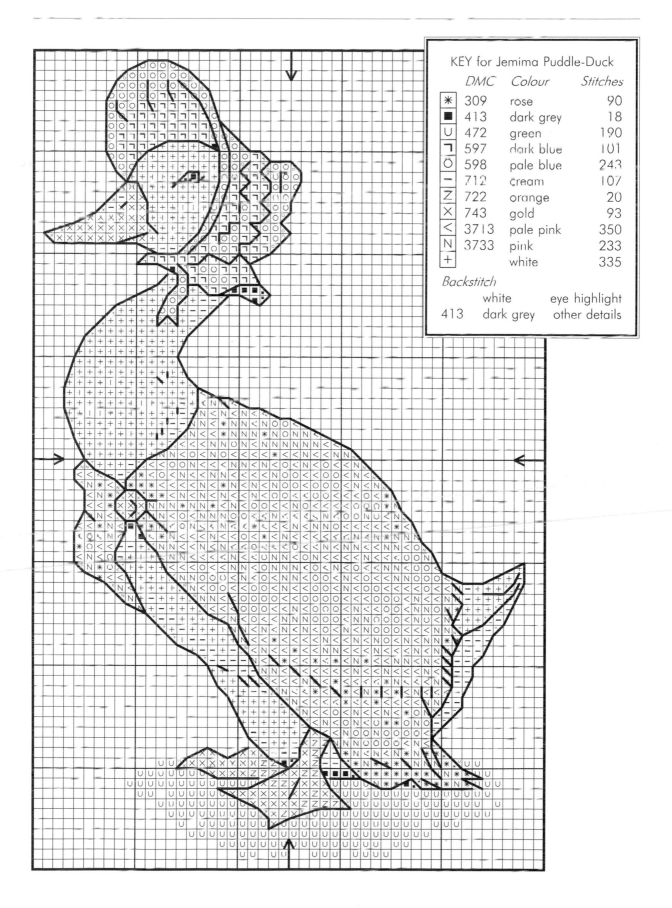

KEY for Jemima Puddle-Duck

	DMC	Colour	Stitches
✱	309	rose	90
■	413	dark grey	18
U	472	green	190
⌐	597	dark blue	101
O	598	pale blue	243
−	712	cream	107
Z	722	orange	20
X	743	gold	93
<	3713	pale pink	350
N	3733	pink	233
+		white	335

Backstitch

	white	eye highlight
413	dark grey	other details

Soft Toy

This Jemima Puddle-Duck jingles when baby shakes her. The pattern is on page 17.

Materials: 28 x 20 cm off-white Aida fabric with 11 thread groups per inch; 28 x 20 cm backing fabric; polyester stuffing; a small bell; DMC embroidery threads listed.

Stitch count: 78H x 47W

Directions: Stitch the design on the Aida fabric. Trim around the design, allowing a 25 mm margin, and zigzag to secure edges. Trim and zigzag backing fabric to match. Lay the two together, right sides facing, and sew around the design, allowing a 1 cm seam, and leaving a gap of several centimetres.

Place a small bell in some polyester stuffing. Turn the toy right side out and fill it with stuffing. Handsew the gap closed.

Baby's Shawl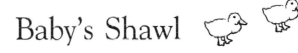

Here a delicate repeat design has been adapted from the pattern on Jemima's own shawl.

Materials: 85 x 85 cm Zweigart Anne fabric (5 x 5 full squares plus a half square all round); DMC embroidery threads listed.

Stitch count: 55H x 55W each square

Directions: Stitch the pattern on alternate squares of the fabric, starting at the central square and stitching thirteen squares to complete. Zigzag around the body of the shawl with white sewing thread. Fray the half-block edges up to the zigzagged line to form a fringe.

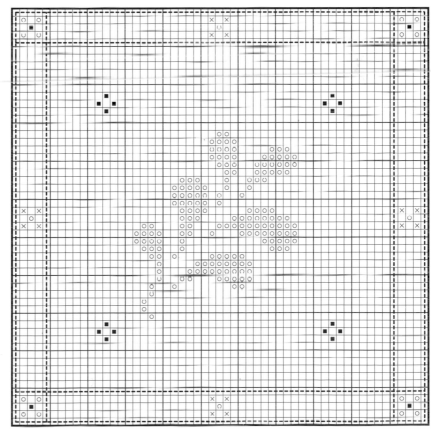

KEY for Baby Shawl		
DMC		Colour
O	598	turquoise
X	3713	pale pink
■	3733	dark pink

Tidy Bag

This pretty carry bag for tissues and other small baby items is pictured on page 22.

Materials: 65 x 25 cm cream linen
with 28 threads per inch;
72 cm of cloth tape or ribbon;
DMC embroidery threads listed.

Stitch count: 49H x 43W

Directions: Zigzag fabric edges to prevent fraying. Sew a 2 cm hem at both of the narrow ends. Stitch the design so that the top starts 7.5 cm below a hemmed edge.

On each hemmed edge of the fabric, mark two points, each 8.5 cm in from the sides. To form the handles, cut two pieces of tape, each 36 cm long, and sew a 2 cm hem at each end. Pin each end of one length of tape onto one of the linen's hemmed edges at the two marked points. Sew around the overlap and diagonally so that the tape is securely attached to the bag. Repeat on the other hemmed edge.

Fold the fabric in half with the design face up and the two hemmed edges aligned. Pin the two layers of fabric at each side, at a point 5 cm up from the folded edge. Turn the front flap over and the bottom flap under so that the design is now inside the bag and there is a valley fold in the base. Sew a 1 cm seam along the two sides. Turn the completed bag right side out. Place a plastic bag inside as a disposable liner.

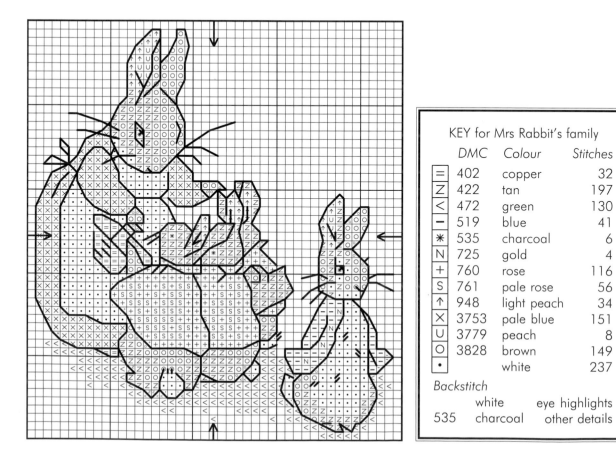

	DMC	Colour	Stitches
=	402	copper	32
Z	422	tan	197
<	472	green	130
−	519	blue	41
✳	535	charcoal	6
N	725	gold	4
+	760	rose	116
S	761	pale rose	56
↑	948	light peach	34
X	3753	pale blue	151
U	3779	peach	8
O	3828	brown	149
•		white	237

KEY for Mrs Rabbit's family

Backstitch

	white	eye highlights
535	charcoal	other details

Birth Record

Hunca Munca and her babies, who feature in The Tale of Two Bad Mice, *make a delightful picture to welcome a new baby - or babies! The chart appears on pages 24-5; the alphabet chart is on page 124.*

Materials: 50 x 50 cm off-white linen
with 25 threads per inch;
sturdy white cardboard;
DMC embroidery threads listed.

Stitch count: 114H x 147W

Directions: If adding a child's name and date of birth below the design, use the alphabet charts to plot out the details. Stitch the full design in the centre of the fabric. Press the work carefully. Cut strong white cardboard to a suitable size. Lay the work over the cardboard, making sure that it is centred. Fold the fabric edges around the board and use strong thread to lace the edges together, side to side and top to bottom.

Fit the covered board into a ready-made frame or have it professionally framed.

	DMC	Colour	Stitches
	KEY for Hunca Munça		
⅟	452	grey	217
X	453	light grey	284
●	517	dark blue	416
–	712	cream	1528
↑	746	pale yellow	944
⌐	760	rose	318
V	761	light rose	1066
U	818	pale pink	96
T	839	dark brown	595
Z	840	brown	773
O	841	light brown	431
<	842	fawn	205
I	948	light peach	648
N	3766	blue-green	456
▲	3779	peach	201
+	3782	mushroom	451
*	3799	charcoal	130
S	3811	pale blue	459
=	3828	tan	347
·		white	1673

Backstitch
760   rose   blanket edging
3799   charcoal   other details

21

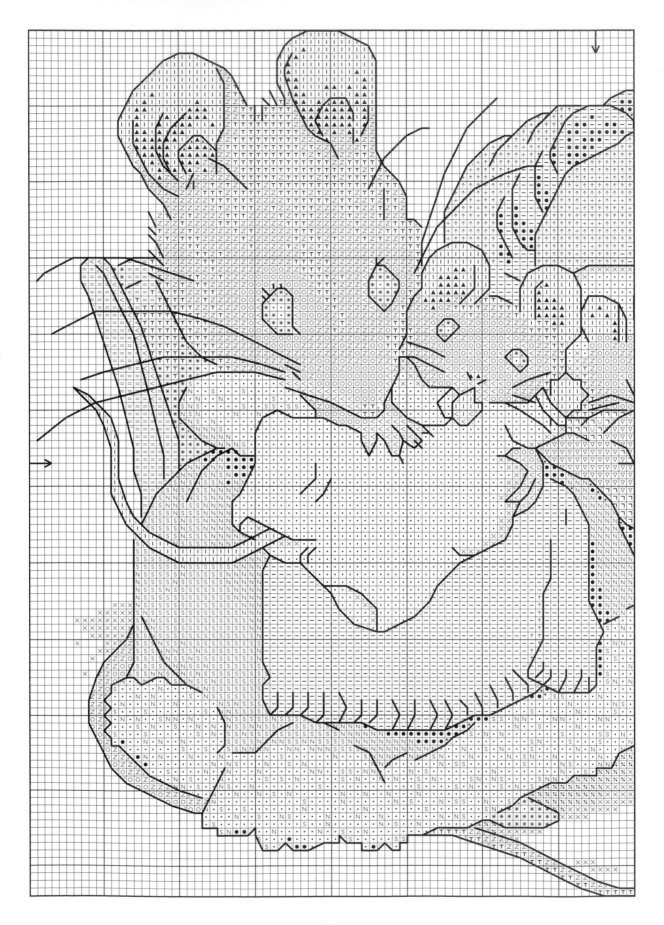

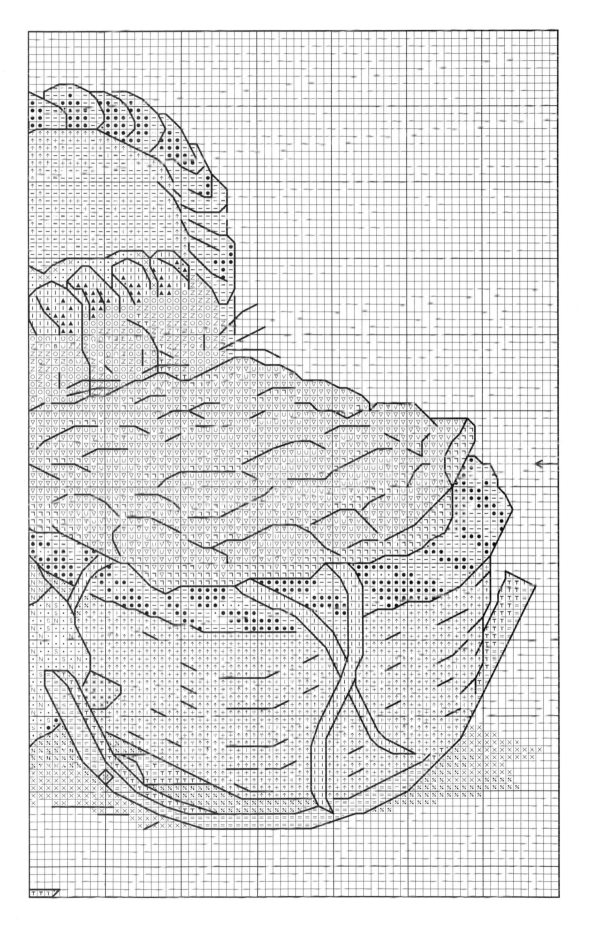

Nutbrown Hares

Before he goes to bed, Little Nutbrown Hare just wants to tell Big Nutbrown Hare how much he loves him: a simple thing perhaps but a very difficult thing to explain. His attempts to measure love provide the story for a wonderful picture book called Guess How Much I Love You which has quickly become a favourite among children (and adults) worldwide. It is a deceptively simple tale, set in woodland with only two characters and told in the time it takes for the moon to rise and for Little Nutbrown Hare to fall asleep. However, the skillful text of author Sam McBratney and the heart-warming illustrations of Anita Jeram ensure that during this short interval, we have all become enchanted.

Play Cubes

The soft blocks on page 26 look delightful and are great fun. You may prefer to put all four designs on different sides of the one block.

Materials: 25 x 25 cm off-white linen
with 28 threads per inch;
white lining fabric;
pastel linen fabrics;
thick foam sponge;
DMC embroidery threads listed.

Stitch count: 42H x 42W each design

Directions: Cut the off-white evenweave linen in four pieces, each 12.5 cm square. Stitch a design on each piece.

Trim the stitched linen squares to 11 cm, back with lining fabric and zigzag the edges. Cut extra 11 cm squares of pastel linen; you will need six fabric squares for each cube.

Lay two squares together, right sides facing, and sew a 1 cm seam along one edge. Open the double section and lay two more squares on top, face down, then sew a seam at each end to form a row of four squares. Add a fifth to form an 'L' shape and a sixth to form a 'T'. Continue sewing seams that join the edges of the squares, creating a box shape, until only three seams remain unsewn. Snip a small triangle off each corner so that the seams will not be too bulky.

Mark and cut 8.5 cm square cubes from a thick sheet of foam sponge, using a serrated knife. Turn the fabric box right side out and insert the foam block. Pin down the flap and handsew the remaining three seams.

KEY for Little Nutbrown Hare			
	DMC	*Colour*	*Stitches*
⌐	435	dark brown	73
O	436	brown	324
X	437	pale brown	568
=	744	yellow	168
▲	966	mint	168
■	3021	chocolate	14
T	3347	dark green	126
U	3348	green	307
<	3752	steel blue	81
↑	3761	blue	168
N	3778	dark peach	31
–	3779	pale peach	233
+		white	421
	3021	chocolate	backstitch

Illustrations © 1994 by Anita Jeram

Cot Bumper

The Nutbrown Hares make perfect company as baby (hopefully) sleeps through the night. The chart can be found on pages 32-3.

Materials: 32 x 42 cm pale blue linen with 25 threads per inch; blue backing fabric; wadding; DMC embroidery threads listed.

Stitch count: 109H x 158W

Directions: Stitch the design in the centre of the evenweave linen. Cut a matching piece of backing fabric.

Make the ties, either in matching fabric as described below or more simply with ribbon. Cut eight strips of fabric, each 40 x 2.5 cm. Press a 5 mm seam along each long edge so that the raw edges almost meet and then press a fold, enclosing the seams inside. Machine or handsew along the fold, tucking in one end for a neat finish.

Lay the embroidered work face up. Measure 4 cm down from the top right corner and position a pair of ties there, with the raw ends aligned to the edge of the linen. Repeat this 4 cm below the top left corner and 4 cm above both of the bottom corners. Lay the backing fabric on top and pin the layers together, securing all the ties. Machine sew a 1 cm seam around the edges, leaving a gap for turning. Turn the bumper right side out.

Cut a 40 x 30 cm piece of wadding and fit it inside the bumper. Near each corner, make a small stitch through all layers to secure the wadding in place. Handsew the opening closed.

	KEY for Hares in the Moonlight		
	DMC	*Colour*	*Stitches*
U	422	pale brown	277
N	445	yellow	50
▲	841	beige	356
–	842	pale beige	711
Z	3045	brown	521
⌐	3347	dark green	1193
O	3348	green	1365
X	3752	blue	253
*	3778	dark peach	31
<	3779	pale peach	64
T	3828	dark brown	317
+		white	1787
	3021	chocolate	backstitch

Illustrations © 1994 by Anita Jeram

Baby's Album

If you prefer to stitch this charming design for framing, you could use a larger count of fabric and omit much of the green foreground. The chart appears overleaf.

Materials: 28 x 35 cm pale blue Aida fabric with 18 thread groups per inch; cream cardboard; thin card; metal screwbinders; tape; DMC embroidery threads listed.

Stitch count: 109H x 160W

Directions: For the sample, white Aida was painted with a blue wash. Stitch the design so that the point indicated by the chart arrows is in the centre of the fabric. Once stitched, trim the Aida to 22 x 30 cm.

From cream cardboard, cut two 25 x 32.5 cm rectangles and two 3 x 32.5 cm strips. Fold a sheet of paper into quarters. Unfold it and trace the pattern below on one quarter. Refold and cut along the arc. Use the paper frame to mark an oval on one cardboard rectangle, then carefully cut along the line with a sharp craft knife. Alternatively, ask a framing shop to cut a suitable mount for you.

On the back of the oval frame, lay pieces of double-sided tape around the window. Position the embroidery carefully in the frame and secure the edges with tape. Cut a 24.5 x 32 cm piece of cardboard, lay double-sided tape around the edges and fix it over the back of the embroidery.

Use strong tape to fix one cardboard strip to the top of the cover, and the other to the top of the back section. For the pages, cut 27 x 31 cm pieces of thin card. Punch three matching holes along the two strips and along the top of each page. Assemble the album—back cover, pages, front cover—and use screwbinders to hold it together.

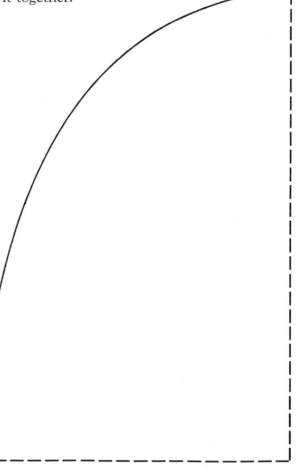

	KEY for Nutbrown Hares		
	DMC	Colour	Stitches
T	435	dark brown	1110
Z	436	brown	3004
U	437	pale brown	1079
■	3021	chocolate	57
–	3347	dark green	866
O	3348	green	3192
X	3752	blue	238
N	3778	dark peach	52
<	3779	pale peach	117
+		white	893
	3021	chocolate	backstitch

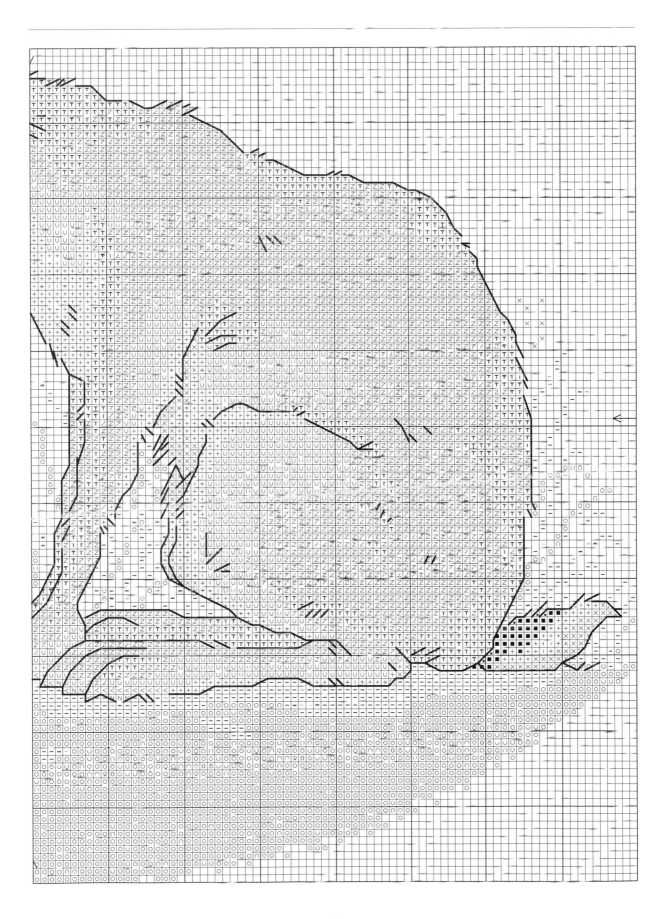

⚘ Gumnut Babies ⚘

Over 80 years ago, a woman called May Gibbs created a world known as Gum-Nut Land, in which the animals and flowers of the Australian bush came very much to life. May was born in England but her family emigrated to Australia when she was a small child. She showed an early talent and studied art in both countries before establishing herself as an illustrator. Gumnut babies appeared in book illustrations from 1913 but it was in 1918, with the publication of Tales of Snugglepot and Cuddlepie, *that May's books caught the public's attention. She wrote thirteen adventures set in Gum-Nut Land in which the real and the imaginary blend delightfully in stories full of excitement and good humour. May's love of the bush changed the way that many felt about native animals and wildflowers.*

Scented Pillow

Shy gumnuts adorn this small pillow, which is pictured on page 39.

Stitch count: 90H x 50W

Directions: Cut the linen in half, each piece measuring 26 x 21 cm, and stitch the design on one. Note: one symbol is worked with a strand of two different colours (sometimes known as 'twilling'). Place the two fabric pieces together with right sides facing. Sew a 1 cm seam, leaving a gap. Turn the pillow right side out. Place a teaspoon of dried lavender in polyester stuffing and push it into the pillow. Handsew the opening closed. Tie a bow with two ribbons and stitch it onto one corner.

Materials: 26 x 42 cm pale blue linen with 28 threads per inch; polyester stuffing; dry lavender; narrow ribbons; DMC threads listed.

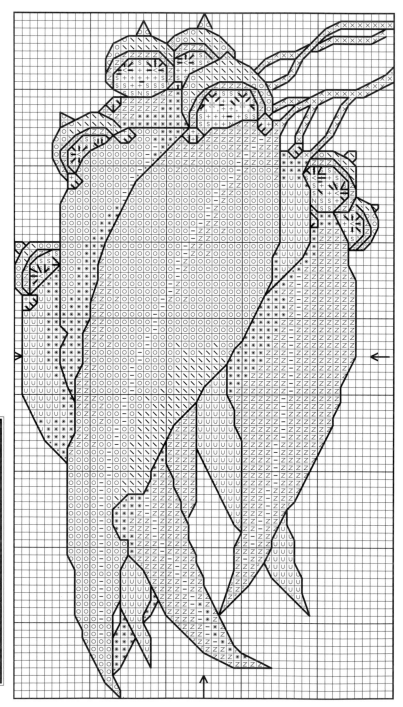

	KEY for the Shy Gumnuts		
	DMC	Colour	Stitches
Z	320	olive	789
N	351	rose	3
✳	501	dark green	287
O	562	green	890
╲	563	mint	180
X	920	rust	81
S	945	apricot	109
+	951	pale apricot	73
<	996	blue	16
−	3823	cream	126
U	320/3042 twilled		257
	838	brown	backstitch

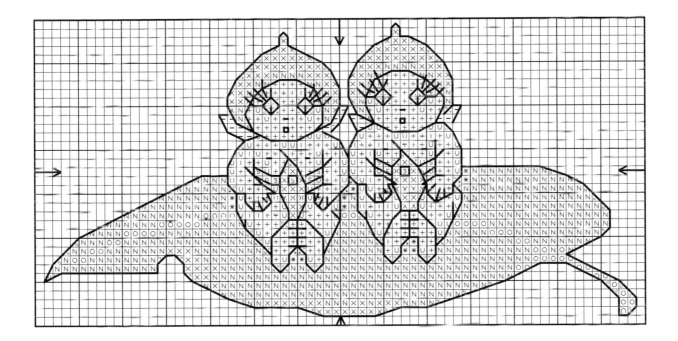

KEY to Snugglepot & Cuddlepie			
	DMC	Colour	Stitches
N	470	dark green	511
X	471	green	145
−	746	pale yellow	17
U	754	peach	118
S	782	brown	11
∗	838	dark brown	18
O	920	rust	55
+	948	light peach	272
•		white	16
Backstitch			
350	rose		mouths
838	dark brown	other details	

Baby Vest

Decorate a baby's garment with this dimpled duo of Snugglepot and Cuddlepie, pictured on page 39.

Materials: 10 x 15 cm waste canvas with 14 threads groups per inch; a cotton vest; DMC embroidery threads listed.

Stitch count: 34H x 68W

Directions: Position the waste canvas on the garment, making sure that it is straight. Tack around the edges and also diagonally so that the canvas is secured to the top layer. Stitch the design, then remove the tacking threads. Dampen the canvas with a clean cloth and carefully pull out the strands of canvas, one at a time.

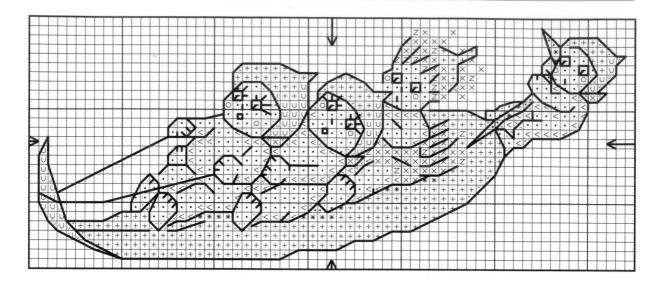

Welcome Card

A cross-stitched card makes a lovely greeting for a new baby: it can then be slipped into a small frame as a keepsake.

Materials: 15 x 20 cm cream linen
with 28 threads per inch;
thin card;
double-sided tape;
DMC embroidery threads listed.

Stitch count: 25H x 63W

Directions: Stitch the design on the fabric and then trim to 11 x 16 cm. Cut an 18 x 39 cm piece of card and score it lightly with a knife to create three equal panels. Trim a narrow strip off the top panel. Cut an 8 x 13 cm window in the centre panel to fit the design. Stick double-sided tape on the inside of the centre panel and position the embroidery so that it is centred in the window. Stick down the top panel as a backing.

	DMC	Colour	Stitches
O	353	dark peach	8
U	470	dark green	55
+	471	green	267
Z	726	gold	15
<	754	peach	107
*	898	dark brown	25
•	948	light peach	272
X	3823	pale yellow	68
−		white	8

KEY for the Gumleaf Ride

Backstitch
352	rose	mouths
898	dark brown	other details

Photo Frame

A whole host of nuts and blossoms decorate this frame for a small photograph, shown on page 43. The dancers could be stitched as single motifs on other items.

Materials: 27 x 23 cm off-white linen
with 25 threads per inch;
sturdy white card;
fray-stop liquid or PVA glue;
double-sided tape;
DMC embroidery threads listed.

Stitch count: 96H x 74W

Directions: Stitch the design on the fabric and careully press the finished work. Cut a 21.5 x 17.5 cm piece of sturdy white card. In the centre, mark and cut a 7 cm square window with a sharp craft knife.

Lay the fabric face down and position the card so that the window frames the cross-stitching. Tape the fabric edges onto the back of the card, folding the corners neatly to reduce bulkiness. Dab some fray-stop liquid or PVA glue onto the fabric at the window corners. When this is dry, make a cut at the centre of the fabric and snip towards each of the corners of the window. Tape the raw edges on the back of the card.

Cut a 21 x 17 cm backing card and glue or tape a suitable photograph in the centre. Glue the front and back of the frame together.

	DMC	Colour	Stitches
	\multicolumn{3}{l}{KEY for Dancing Blossoms}

	DMC	Colour	Stitches
Z	351	rose	70
U	353	dark peach	31
X	726	yellow	172
<	754	peach	268
N	906	green	99
O	907	light green	42
+	948	light peach	415
−	3823	pale yellow	495
•		white	4

Backstitch

782	tan	yellow blossom
817	red	red blossom
838	dark brown	other details

© Copyright TNS and SCNSW

44

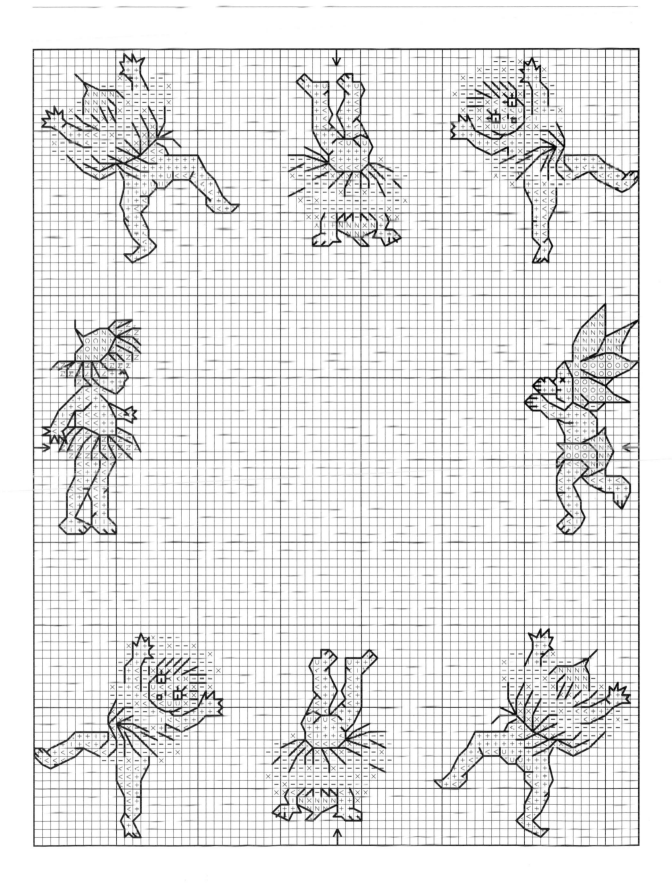

Little Mites

*The first few years
are filled with discoveries about
the world around us and also
about ourselves. There's a little of
Pinocchio in all of us, although
our noses may not give us away
quite so dramatically. There's also
a lot of Kipper's endless curiosity
and Frog's sense of importance.
Along with Old Bear and his
furry friends, these characters
make wonderful companions
through the toddler years.*

Pinocchio

It's no coincidence that books for the very young are filled with animals and that human beings only start to appear in those written for older children. The tale of Pinocchio, the wooden puppet who becomes a child, is one that fits somewhere in the middle. It's a story about growing up: the naughty marionette, created by old Geppetto, gets into all manner of troubles and is rescued by the wise cricket and the blue-haired fairy many times before he reaches his goal and becomes a real boy. Possibly one of the world's greatest shaggy dog stories, The Adventures of Pinocchio was written by Carlo Collodi (although his real name was Lorenzini). Collodi was a 19th century Italian journalist who wrote the tale to pay off his gambling debts. His book, halfway between a fairy tale and a bizarre newspaper story, struck a chord with growing children everywhere and is justly considered a classic of children's literature.

Framed Picture

The blue-haired fairy tells young Pinocchio a few home truths in this scene, which makes a sweet framed picture. The chart is on page 49.

Materials: 30 x 27 cm white linen
with 28 threads per inch;
sturdy white cardboard;
coloured card;
DMC embroidery threads listed.

Stitch count: 94H x 75W

Directions: Stitch the design on the fabric and carefully press the finished work.

Cut a 26 x 22 cm piece of sturdy white card and lay the stitched work over the cardboard, making sure that it is centred. Fold the fabric edges around the board and use strong thread to lace the edges together, side to side and top to bottom.

Cut two 27 x 23 cm pieces of coloured card. On one, mark and cut a 21 x 17 cm window. Lay double-sided tape around the window area on the back of the frame and position it over the embroidery. Glue or use double-sided tape to fix the backing card over the lacing.

Use a hole punch to cut numerous spots from card of a contrasting colour. Arrange and glue these on the front of the frame.

KEY for Pinocchio & the Fairy			
	DMC	Colour	Stitches
T	317	dark grey	1
X	350	rose	192
▲	353	peach	7
U	743	yellow	311
–	744	pale yellow	990
<	948	light peach	303
↑	955	pale green	305
O	964	mint	301
Z	976	brown	223
4	3753	pale blue	409
⌐	3826	dark brown	108
N	3827	light brown	245
+		white	29
	317	dark grey	backstitch

Towel Trim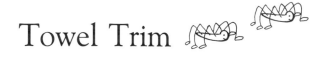

Children can see Pinocchio's nose grow before their very eyes on this trim, ideal for a towel or a bedsheet. It is pictured on page 54.

Materials: A handtowel;
3"-wide white Aida band
with 15 thread groups per inch;
DMC embroidery threads listed.

Stitch count: 36H (width is adaptable)

Directions: Cut a strip of Aida band 4 cm wider than the width of the towel and stitch the figures onto it so that they are well spaced. Tack the strip onto your towel and then slipstitch along the edges, turning the ends under neatly. Press the towel carefully to complete.

Feeding Bib

This useful item is pictured on page 55.

Materials: 25 x 30 cm cream Aida fabric
with 14 thread groups per inch;
25 x 30 cm lining fabric;
2 m bias binding;
DMC embroidery threads listed.

Stitch count: 44H x 68W

Directions: Draw the 23 x 28 cm bib shape on paper, using the pattern on page 126 as a guide. Make sure the neck is large enough to fit the baby comfortably. Mark the shape onto the Aida and stitch the design in the lower half of the fabric.
Cut the Aida and lining fabric to shape. Zigzag the fabric edges together. Trim the outside edges with folded bias binding. Pin a 1 m strip of bias binding around the neckline so that the ties are of even length. Starting at one tie end, sew along the folded bias binding, continue around the neckline and to the end of the other tie.

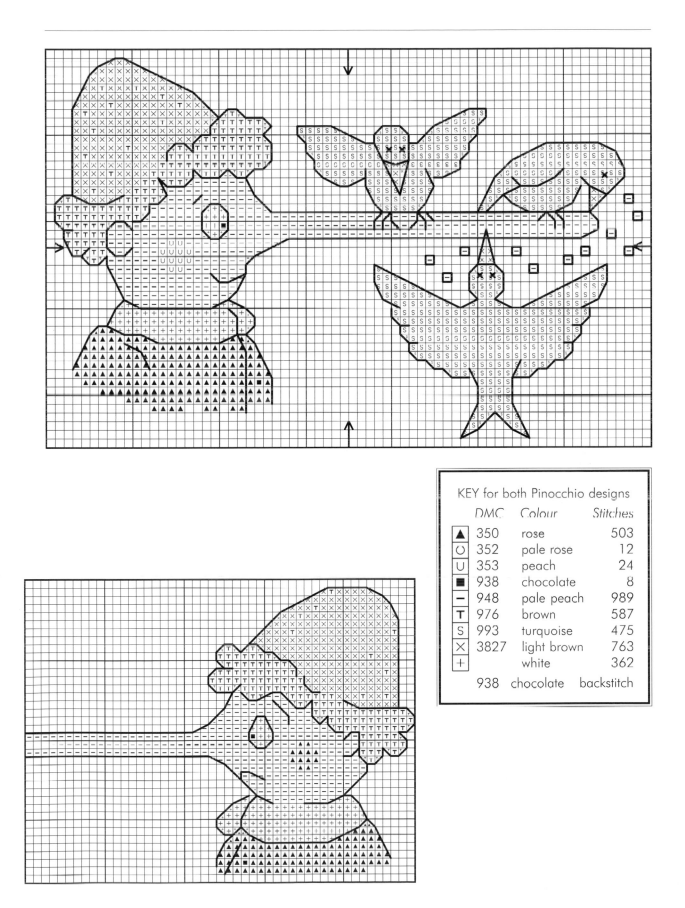

KEY for both Pinocchio designs

	DMC	Colour	Stitches
▲	350	rose	503
♡	352	pale rose	12
U	353	peach	24
■	938	chocolate	8
−	948	pale peach	989
T	976	brown	587
S	993	turquoise	475
×	3827	light brown	763
+		white	362

938   chocolate   backstitch

Everyone knows what happens to
Pinocchio's nose, shown here on a
towel trim. The chart is on page 52.

Pinocchio's nose returns to size,
whittled away by woodpeckers.
Instructions for making this bib
appear on page 52-3.

Pyjama Case

Pinocchio's flight on a dove decorates a case which can hold all kinds of things, including pyjamas. It is shown on page 47.

Materials: 37 x 76 cm blue Aida fabric with 14 thread groups per inch; lining fabric; snap fasteners; DMC embroidery threads listed.

Stitch count: 63H x 74W (each panel)

Directions: Orient the fabric so that the 37 cm edges are top and bottom. Stitch the design so that it begins 20 cm from the top edge. Press the finished work carefully.

Fold the fabric in half, right sides facing, and sew a 1 cm seam down each side. Turn over the bag opening and sew a 2 cm hem.

Cut a 37 x 76 cm piece of lining fabric,

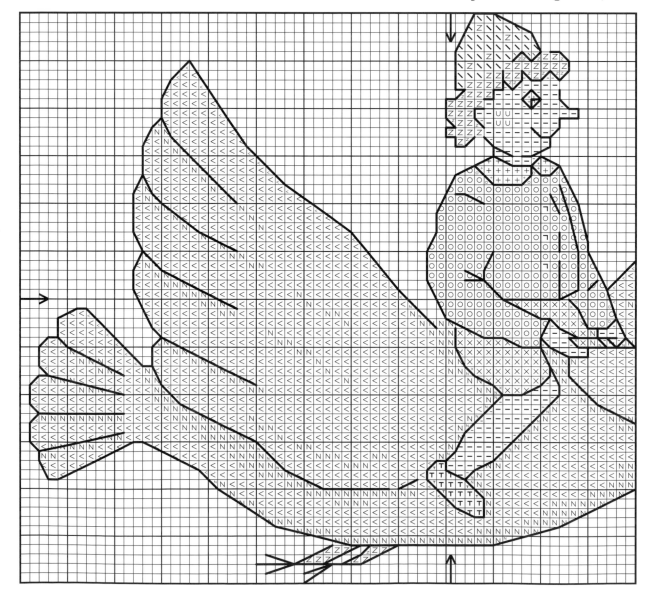

fold it in half and seam the sides to form a matching bag. Insert the lining bag, wrong side out, into the Aida bag. Turn in the raw edge of the lining bag and slipstitch it neatly onto the Aida.

Inside the bag near the opening, neatly sew a single snap fastener. Fold down the top of the bag to form an 8 cm flap. Under the flap, 3 cm in from each side, position a snap fastener and sew them both in place.

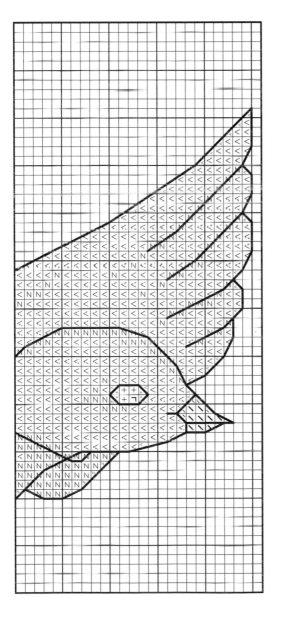

KEY for Pinocchio's flight			
	DMC	Colour	Stitches
⌐	317	dark grey	5
O	350	rose	255
U	353	peach	4
—	948	pale peach	140
X	964	turquoise	67
Z	976	brown	64
N	3042	mauve	441
<	3743	pale mauve	1759
T	3826	dark brown	21
\	382/	light brown	53
+		white	28

Backstitch
964   turquoise   reins
317   dark grey   other details

Kipper

This delightful young dog first appeared in a minor role in the award-winning book The Blue Balloon. Kipper demanded (and soon got) a string of his very own books beginning, of course, with Kipper. These have been a great success and have so far been translated into more than a dozen languages. Kipper's naivety and curiosity inevitably lead to mild havoc and the raised eyebrow that he wears indicates a state of perpetual surprise at the minutiae of everyday life. His talented creator is Mick Inkpen, who has given us a whole cast of wonderful book characters, including Wibbly Pig, Penguin Small and Threadbear. However, it is Kipper who has reached the giddy heights of superstardom, making the leap from the printed page onto the television screen while remaining the unassuming pup that he is.

Bathroom Tidy

Make a hanging tidy to hold all those bits and pieces for a child's bath. This one, shown on page 58, features Kipper and his gosling friend.

Materials: 48 x 30 cm white Aida fabric with 14 thread groups per inch; white lining fabric; bias binding; ribbon; thin dowel; DMC embroidery threads listed.

Stitch count: 63H x 110W each figure

Directions: Cut a 10 x 30 cm strip of Aida fabric, leaving a 38 x 30 cm piece for the base. Orient the base piece so that the 38 cm edges are at the sides and stitch the design 7 cm from the top edge.

Cut a matching piece of lining fabric and lay it on the stitched work, right sides facing. Sew a 1 cm seam around all edges, leaving a small gap for turning. Trim the corners, turn right side out and sew the gap closed. Fold the top edge over 3 cm and sew across 2 cm from the fold to make a casing for the dowel.

Lay the Aida strip so that the long edges are top and bottom. Measure and mark 3.5 cm in from each bottom edge. Trim from each mark to the top corners, creating a boat shape. Sew bias binding around the edges. Pin this onto the base fabric with the sides vertical so that it forms a pocket. Sew the sides and bottom onto the base fabric.

Cut a 35 cm length of thin dowel. Thread the dowel through the casing. Cut 55 cm of ribbon and tie each end to a dowel end to form a hanging loop.

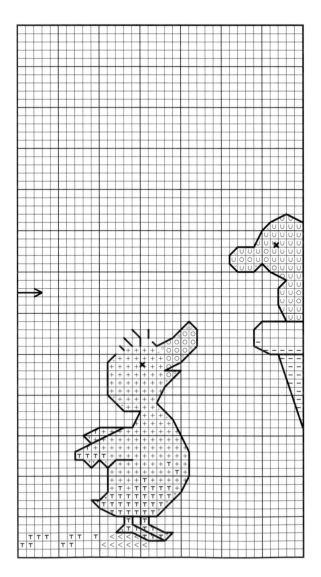

	DMC	Colour	Stitches		DMC	Colour	Stitches
T	535	grey	73	<	3747	pale blue	165
O	725	gold	40	+		white	508
U	726	yellow	117	−		ecru	467
X	809	blue	77				
ㄱ	869	brown	61	Backstitch			
‖	976	tan	175			white	nose highlight
N	977	light tan	145		535	grey	other details
■	3021	dark brown	74				

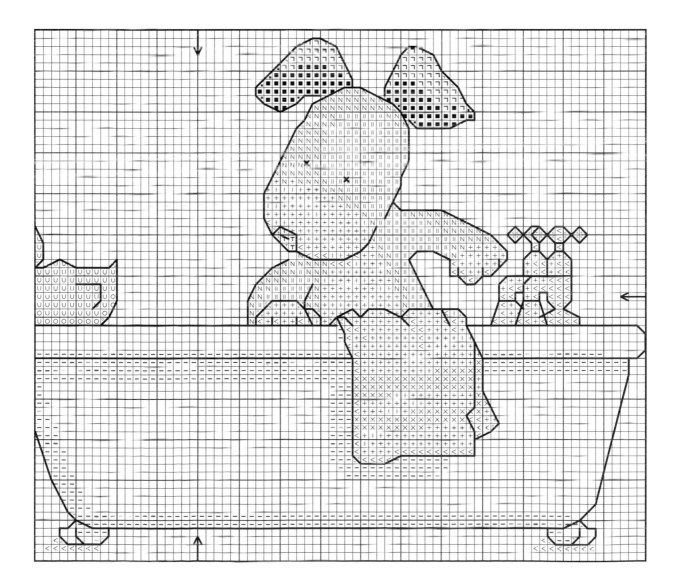

Sunhat

Kipper, along with bucket and spade, is the perfect companion for a day at the beach.

Materials: 15 x 12 cm white Aida fabric with 14 thread groups per inch; 30 cm x 1 m white cotton fabric; iron-on interfacing; a large button; DMC embroidery threads listed.

Stitch count: 38H x 33W

Directions: Trace the patterns for the panel and brim (found on page 126) onto paper and cut templates. Adding a 1 cm seam allowance, cut the panel nine times from white cotton and cut the brim twice, making sure it is on the fabric fold.

Using the paper template, mark the panel outline on the Aida with running stitches.

Stitch the design so it starts 1 cm from the baseline of the panel. When complete, trim the panel 1 cm outside the running stitches.

With right sides facing, sew five plain panel pieces together for the inner crown and five (including the Aida panel) for the outer crown. Press seams.

Iron interfacing onto one brim piece and trim excess. Lay the two brim pieces together with right sides facing and sew the outside edge. Turn right side out and topstitch the outside edge. Sew the outer crown and brim together, right sides facing, along the raw edges. Place the inner crown inside the cap with wrong sides facing. Turn under a 1 cm hem all round and handsew it in place. Sew a large button on top of the hat, through both layers.

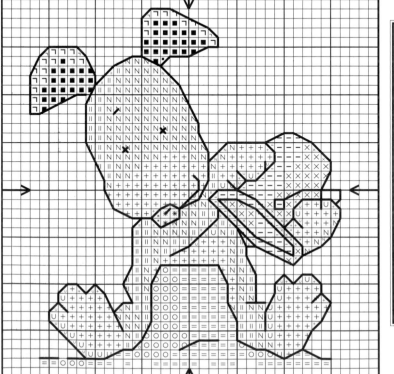

KEY for Kipper at the beach			
	DMC	Colour	Stitches
X	518	sea blue	46
−	519	pale sea blue	55
✳	535	grey	5
O	725	gold	41
˥	869	brown	27
‖	976	tan	80
N	977	light tan	152
■	3021	dark brown	44
U	3747	pale blue	40
=	3822	pale gold	81
+		white	174

Backstitch

	white	nose highlight
535	grey	other details

Cushion

This project, seen on page 63, offers some charming indoor company, no matter what the weather.

Materials: 21 x 21 cm white linen
with 28 threads per inch;
pale blue cotton;
white lining cotton;
a cushion pad or filler;
DMC embroidery threads listed.

Stitch count: 87H x 75W

Directions: Stitch the design in the centre of the linen square. Cut a matching piece of white lining fabric and baste the two pieces together, wrong sides facing, around the edges.

Cut four pieces from the coloured fabric, each measuring 10 x 37 cm. Lay one strip on an edge of the linen, right sides facing, and sew a 1 cm seam. Repeat with the remaining three strips. Fold the ends of the strips to create a neat mitre at each corner. Baste and sew each mitre. Trim and press the seams.

Line this front section with more white lining fabric. If you choose, you might like to sew a large button at each corner of the centre panel.

Cut backing fabric to match the cushion front. Lay the front and back sections together, right sides facing. Sew around three sides, allowing a 1 cm seam. Snip away excess fabric at the corners. Turn the cushion right sides out and press a 1 cm seam at the open edge. Insert the cushion pad or filler and slipstitch the opening closed.

© MI 1999

	KEY for Kipper in the rain		
	DMC	Colour	Stitches
<	353	pink	8
T	535	grey	36
Z	642	fawn	104
X	809	blue	325
⌐	869	brown	70
▲	976	tan	97
N	977	light tan	487
■	3021	dark brown	42
O	3024	pale grey	598
↑	3747	pale blue	118
−	3822	gold	21
+		white	1045
U		ecru	112

Backstitch
white   nose highlight
535   grey   other details

Old Bear & Friends

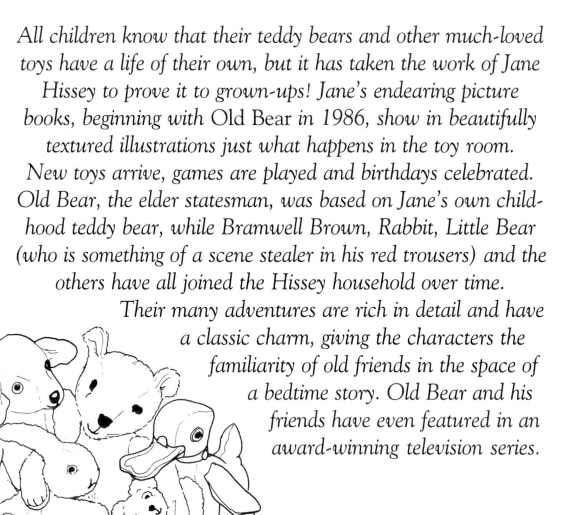

All children know that their teddy bears and other much-loved toys have a life of their own, but it has taken the work of Jane Hissey to prove it to grown-ups! Jane's endearing picture books, beginning with Old Bear in 1986, show in beautifully textured illustrations just what happens in the toy room. New toys arrive, games are played and birthdays celebrated. Old Bear, the elder statesman, was based on Jane's own childhood teddy bear, while Bramwell Brown, Rabbit, Little Bear (who is something of a scene stealer in his red trousers) and the others have all joined the Hissey household over time. Their many adventures are rich in detail and have a classic charm, giving the characters the familiarity of old friends in the space of a bedtime story. Old Bear and his friends have even featured in an award-winning television series.

Doorplate

The parade of toys on page 67 leads the way into a child's bedroom. If you wish to add a name below the animals, you'll need to adjust the measurements given.

Materials: 20 x 35 cm green Aida fabric
with 11 thread groups per inch;
sturdy white cardboard;
strong coloured cardboard;
ribbon;
DMC embroidery threads listed.

Stitch count: 55H x 120W

Directions: For the sample, white Aida fabric was painted with a pale green wash.

Stitch the design on the Aida, using three strands for the cross-stitch and two for backstitches. Stitch the string in the picture with long stitches.

Cut a 16 x 30 cm piece of white cardboard and position the embroidery over it. Fold the edges of the fabric over and tape them onto the back. Lace the top and bottom edges with strong thread, then lace the two side edges.

Cut a 20 x 34 cm piece of coloured card. Tape or staple a length of ribbon onto this backing panel for hanging. Fix the laced embroidery onto the backing card with glue or double-sided tape.

KEY for the Toy Parade

	DMC	Colour	Stitches
■	310	black	147
I	352	dark peach	25
\	353	peach	45
=	356	rust	216
S	422	fawn	163
●	606	red	63
<	676	sand	238
—	677	straw	205
L	702	green	19
Z	740	orange	96
∩	742	gold	27
I	744	yellow	118
→	754	pale peach	108
⌐	781	brown	313
X	783	light brown	110
▲	794	pale blue	45
T	798	blue	139
◆	645	charcoal	22
✳	920	red-brown	160
N	992	dark turquoise	46
U	993	turquoise	25
+	3778	liver	365
↑	3813	mint	221
•		white	129
O		ecru	241

Backstitch

310	black	bear noses & claws Sailor's & Zebra's eyes
606	red	Sailor's mouth
677	straw	string
740	orange	eyes of Rabbit, Little Bear & Bramwell
744	yellow	Duck's seams
	white	Zebra's hair
645	charcoal	other details

Pencil Pot

The excitable Little Bear makes a wonderful motif that is quick to stitch.

Materials: 3"-wide white Aida band
with 15 thread groups per inch;
a jar or tin;
DMC embroidery threads listed.

Stitch count: 38H x 33W

Directions: Select a suitable jar or tin and make sure it is clean and dry. Measure its circumference and cut a length of Aida band 2 cm longer. Stitch the design in the centre.

Zigzag the raw edges of the band to prevent fraying. Fold the band in half, right sides facing, with the two zigzagged edges together and sew a 1 cm seam. Turn the band right side out and slip it onto the jar, making sure that the seams lie flat.

KEY for Little Bear			
	DMC	Colour	Stitches
■	310	black	3
=	422	brown	90
N	433	dark brown	22
X	606	red	241
O	608	orange	15
+	677	straw	273
T	817	dark red	54

Backstitch

310	black	eyes, nose, mouth
433	dark brown	fur
817	dark red	trousers

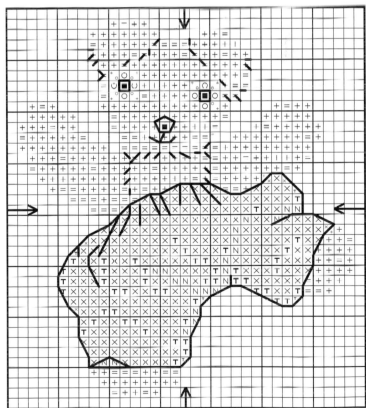

Alphabet Sampler

Old Bear and many of his friends add their charm to the alphabet in this lovely sampler, pictured on page 75.

Materials: 55 x 55 cm off-white linen with 25 threads per inch; white board or heavy card stock; DMC embroidery threads listed.

Stitch count: 180H x 180W

Directions: Stitch the design and carefully press the finished work.

Cut strong white board to a suitable size. Lay the work over the board and make sure that it is centred. Fold the edges of the fabric around the board and use a strong thread to lace the edges together: side to side and top to bottom. Fit the covered board into a ready-made frame or have it professionally framed.

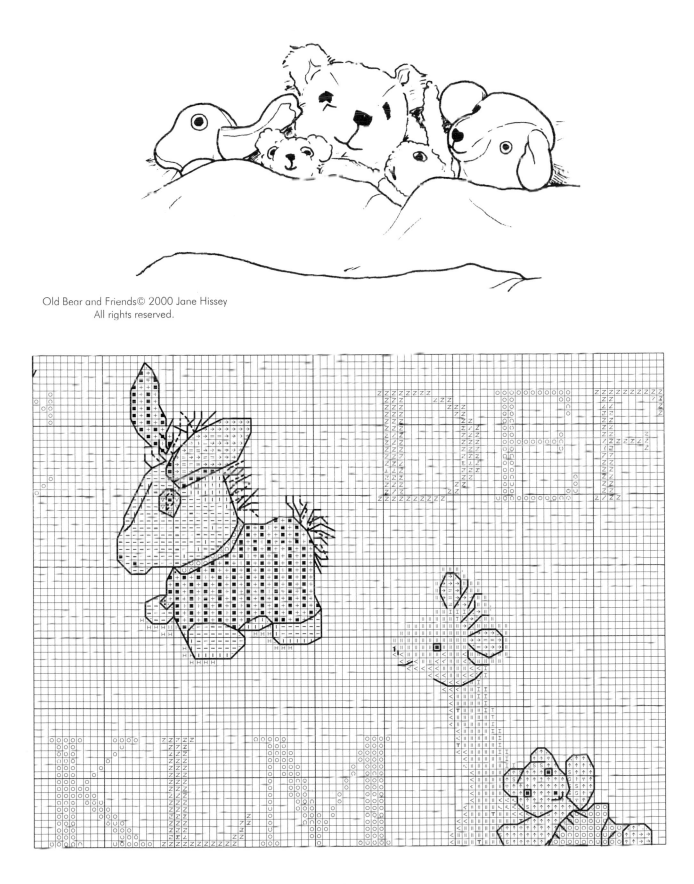

Old Bear and Friends© 2000 Jane Hissey

KEY for Toy Alphabet

	DMC	Colour	Stitches
■	310	black	253
∩	352	dark peach	20
=	353	peach	26
▲	356	rust	262
S	422	fawn	398
O	606	red	1303
H	647	grey	155
＼	676	sand	134
I	677	straw	486
✳	702	green	24
↑	739	pale brown	1359
▽	740	orange	262
I	741	light orange	167
<	743	yellow	329
‖	744	pale yellow	582
→	754	pale peach	244
◆	780	dark brown	310
T	781	dark tan	509
X	783	tan	129
Z	798	dark blue	1486
L	920	red-brown	49
N	992	dark turquoise	194
U	993	turquoise	19
⁒	3778	liver	554
+		white	379
–		ecru	704

Backstitch

310   black Little Bear's mouth, Old Bear's eyes, nose & claws, Bramwell's nose, mouth & claws, Sailor's eyes & nose, Hoot's apron pocket

606   red   Sailor's mouth

741   orange   Little Bear's eye

780   dark brown   Bramwell, Hoot's eye outline

783   tan   Duck's seams

992   turquoise Jolly Tall's eye   white   Camel's eye, Zebra's inner eye & hair, eye highlight for Hoot & Bramwell

645   charcoal   other details

Alphabet Characters

Hoot the owl
Zebra
Bramwell Brown
Jolly Tall the giraffe
  & Little Bear
Sailor & Duck
Rabbit
Camel
Old Bear

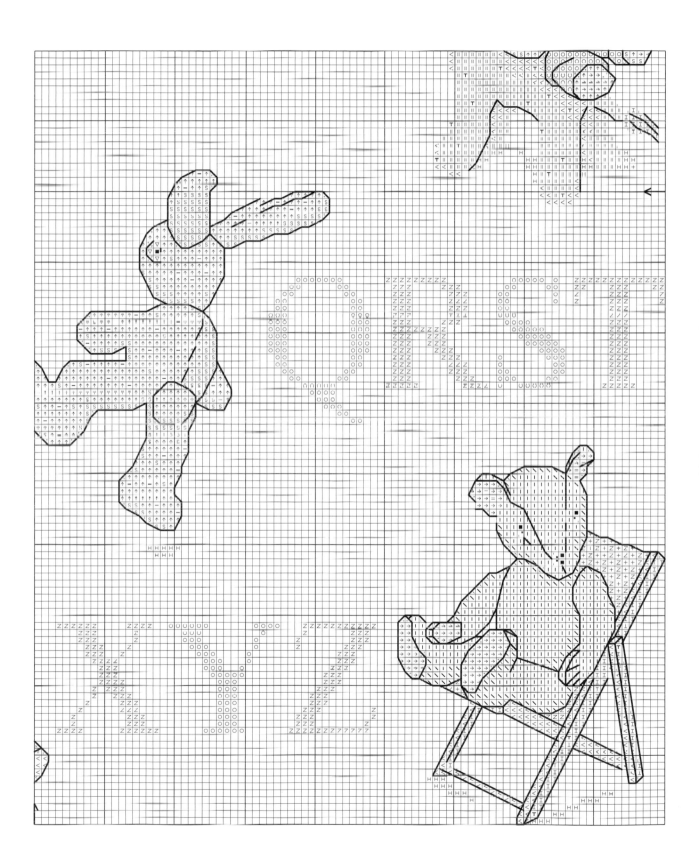

Frog

Here is a hero who is extremely easy to identify with: he is often a bit silly and sometimes even a little scared. This imperfect but very lovable character is the creation of the Dutch author and illustrator Max Velthuijs. Frog lives in beautiful countryside of rolling hills and picturesque lakes with his good friends, Duck, Hare and Pig (and sometimes Rat, who is a bit of a wanderer). Their adventures are gentle tales about the strength of friendship, the value of the individual (delightfully resolved in the philosophical Frog Is Frog), and the rhythm of the seasons. These are illustrated with charming works of art in which Frog's whole inner life can be read in the line of his mouth. Over a million copies of books about Frog have been sold throughout some twenty-five countries.

Boating Bag

This drawstring bag is ideal for storing socks or handkerchiefs or even for carrying on a special outing.

Materials: 30 x 68 cm pale blue linen with 28 threads per inch; white lining fabric; 1 m piping cord; DMC embroidery threads listed.

Stitch count: 55H x 83W

Directions: Fold the linen in half to form a rectangle with a 30 cm top and base. Stitch the design so that the lower edge is 35 mm up from the folded base.

Fold the linen with right sides facing and sew a 1 cm seam up both sides, leaving a 2 cm gap in the stitching 5 cm from the top edges. Sew a matching piece of lining fabric in the same way. Trim the corners of both bags. Turn the linen bag right side out and insert the lining bag. Turn the opening of both bags in 1 cm and handsew the lining to the linen bag around the neck. At 4 cm below the opening, stitch a horizontal seam through the linen and the lining of one side and then the other side. Stitch a parallel line 2 cm above this.

Cut the cord into two equal lengths. Thread a piece of cord through the channel on each side of the bag and knot the ends at either edge.

KEY for Frog & Duck boating			
	DMC	Colour	Stitches
N	351	rose	30
+	702	dark green	191
U	703	green	41
O	741	orange	20
T	772	pale green	411
Z	782	brown	45
X	813	smoky blue	160
✱	844	dark grey	63
▲	912	emerald	77
S	995	dark blue	174
<	996	blue	357
–	3761	pale blue	366
↑	3821	sand	264
•		white	393
Backstitch			
702	dark green	flower stem	
844	dark grey	other details	

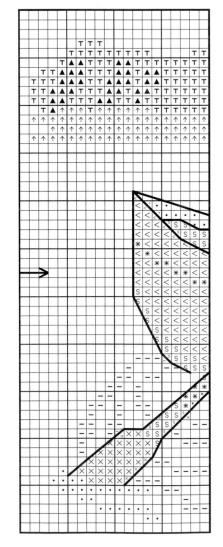

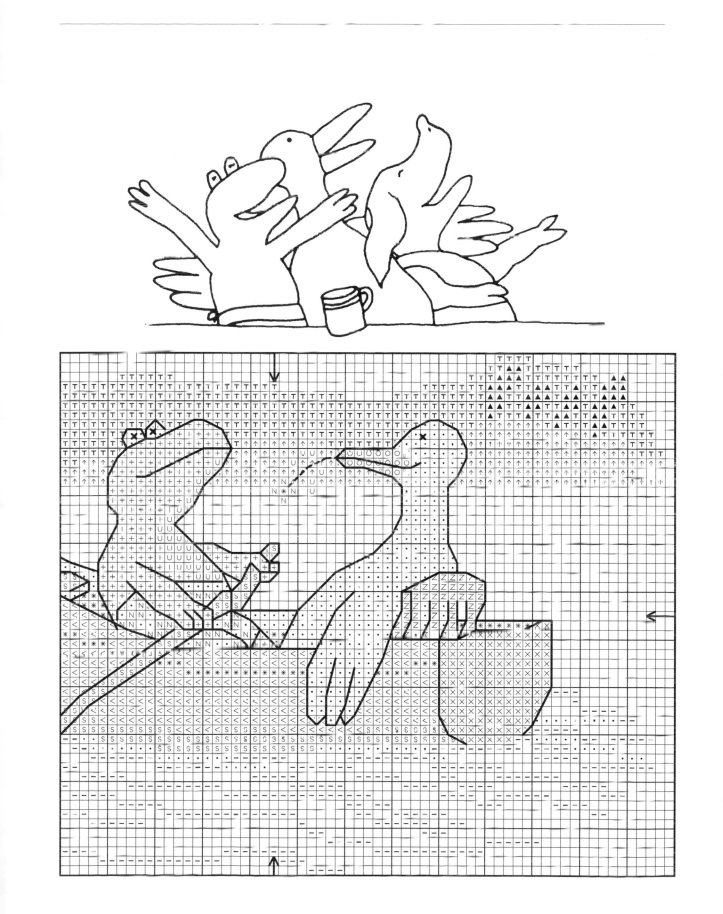

T-shirt

Frog, in one of his most endearing moments, makes a bold statement for a child to wear.

Materials: 15 x 15 cm waste canvas
with 10 thread groups per inch;
a white t-shirt or top;
DMC embroidery threads listed.

Stitch count: 53H x 52W

Directions: Position the waste canvas on the front of the top, ensuring that it is squared up. Tack around the edges and also diagonally so that the canvas is securely attached to the fabric.

Cross-stitch with three strands of thread and backstitch with two. Remove the tacking threads and dampen the canvas with a cloth. Slowly pull out the strands of the waste canvas, one at a time. Carefully press the finished garment.

KEY for Frog with wings			
	DMC	Colour	Stitches
+	351	rose	83
O	702	dark green	287
X	703	green	91
■	844	dark grey	4
▲	922	orange	55
T	976	brown	315
U	3753	blue	115
–	3756	pale blue	466
•		white	101

Backstitch
703	green	grass
413	dark grey	other details

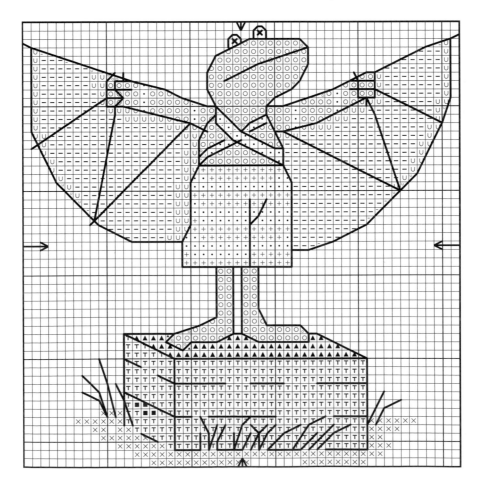

Season Sampler

These charming scenes of the year's changes could be stitched as individual pieces, or as part of the picture shown on pages 86-7.

Materials: 45 x 40 cm white Aida fabric with 14 thread groups per inch; white board or heavy card stock; DMC embroidery threads listed.

Stitch count: 63H x 74W (each panel)

Directions: Stitch the four panel designs, leaving a gap of six rows between them.

Cut strong white board to a suitable size. Lay the work over the board and make sure that it is centred. Fold the edges of the fabric around the board and use a strong thread to lace the edges together: side to side and top to bottom.

Fit the covered board into a ready-made frame or have it professionally framed.

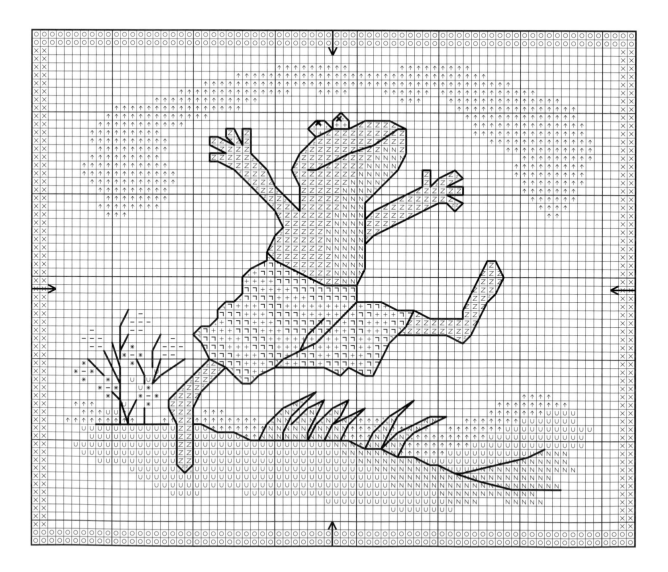

KEY for Frog in Spring			
	DMC	Colour	Stitches
O	210	purple	296
X	211	light purple	236
⌐	351	rose	140
Z	702	dark green	297
N	704	green	267
✳	799	blue	16
–	973	yellow	22
↑	3/47	light blue	540
U	3819	light green	341
+		white	114

Backstitch

704	green	grass
814	dark grey	other details

KEY for Hare in Summer			
	DMC	Colour	Stitches
4	350	rose	57
Z	760	pink	29
<	799	dark blue	296
↑	827	blue	544
T	844	dark grey	2
U	911	dark green	155
■	913	green	563
–	973	yellow	175
N	976	brown	286
+	977	light brown	68
X	3747	light blue	236
▲		white	/

844	dark grey	backstitch

KEY for Pig in Autumn

	DMC	Colour	Stitches
✳	301	dark brown	188
✕	351	rose	479
=	402	apricot	236
N	469	dark green	85
U	471	green	532
O	518	blue	339
Z	760	pink	5
■	761	pale pink	188
4	973	yellow	80
<	977	tan	551
⊥	3072	grey	308
+		white	58
	844	dark grey	backstitch

88

105

Growing Years

The stories that appeal to older children tend to be about people rather than animals and this section features some of the best loved ones: Dorothy from the Land of Oz, the ever-wandering Wally, and the charming Little Prince. They appear on an array of unusual projects and gifts which are certain to delight youngsters.

The Wizard of Oz

The tale of a small girl picked up by a cyclone and deposited in the magical land of Oz has been a favourite with children for a whole century. Lyman Frank Baum was an enterprising American who, having tried his hand at retailing, the theatre, newspaper work, poultry farming and even manufacturing axle grease, took up the pen and wrote books for children. His first original story, called The Wizard of Oz, was published in 1900 and was an instant success, inspiring a stage musical and, much later, the famous film. It is the story of Dorothy and her dog Toto, who must make a difficult journey to meet the Wizard of Oz so they can return home to Kansas. Along the way, they meet the Scarecrow, the Tin Woodman and the Cowardly Lion, each of whom join the quest to the Emerald City. Although this remained the best known, Baum wrote a further thirteen books about the Land of Oz.

Finger Puppets

With puppets of Dorothy, Toto, Glinda the Good Witch, a Munchkin, the Scarecrow, the Woodman, the Lion, and the Wizard himself, children can act out all the Oz stories.

Materials: 12 x 64 cm white Aida fabric with 14 thread groups per inch; 24 x 64 cm white lining fabric; 12 x 64 cm coloured fabric; DMC embroidery threads listed.

Stitch count: approximately 40H x 20W

Directions: Stitch each figure on a 12 x 8 cm piece of Aida fabric. For each puppet, cut two 12 x 8 cm pieces of lining fabric and one of coloured fabric.

Lay each stitched figure face down on a lining piece and sew along the base, 5 mm below the bottom row of cross-stitches. Trim the edge and zigzag it, then turn the piece inside out so that the design faces out and is backed with the white fabric. Tack 5 mm around the figure, stitching the layers together.

Sew the other lining piece and the coloured piece together along one edge, forming the base. Trim the edge and zigzag, then turn the piece inside out. Place the two sections together with the bases aligned and with the cross-stitching and coloured fabric facing each other. Sew them together, using the basted outline as a guide. Trim the edges and zigzag. Turn the puppet right side out, using a teaspoon to ease them into shape.

To make a puppet stand, drill holes in a narrow block of timber and glue in short sections of dowel.

	DMC	Colour	Stitches
▼	301	red-brown	377
●	350	red	113
\	415	light grey	48
S	437	light brown	45
■	535	dark grey	245
T	646	grey	71
U	702	dark green	69
X	704	green	289
↑	744	yellow	31
–	754	peach	241
Z	798	dark blue	305
⌐	809	blue	496
<	972	gold	489
N	976	brown	62
I	3072	silver-grey	411
O	3747	pale blue	114
+		white	433
•	5283	metallic silver	53
	535	dark grey	backstitch

KEY for Land of Oz friends

Trim

The Queen of the Mice and her two subjects are small enough to be stitched on almost anything, including the trim shown overleaf.

Materials: 2"-wide cream Aida band with 15 thread groups per inch; DMC embroidery threads listed.

Stitch count: 20H (width is adaptable)

Directions: Cut a length of Aida band suitable for your purpose: perhaps for a serviette ring or a band to fit around a pin cushion. Stitch the figures onto it so that they are evenly spaced.

KEY for Mice			
	DMC	Colour	Stitches
X	353	peach	75
+	725	yellow	11
•		white	248
	413	charcoal	backstitch

Child's Top

That much-loved Oz trio–the Scarecrow, the Tin Woodman and the Cowardly Lion– head off to find their heart's desire in the design shown overleaf.

Materials: 14 x 20 cm waste canvas with 11 thread groups per inch; a sweatshirt or other garment; DMC embroidery threads listed.

Stitch count: 48H x 75W

Directions: Position the waste canvas on the front of the top, ensuring that it is squared up. Tack around the edges and also diagonally so that the canvas is securely attached to the fabric.

Cross-stitch with three strands of thread and backstitch with two. Remove the tacking threads and dampen the canvas with a cloth. Slowly pull out the strands of the waste canvas, one at a time. Carefully press the finished garment if necessary.

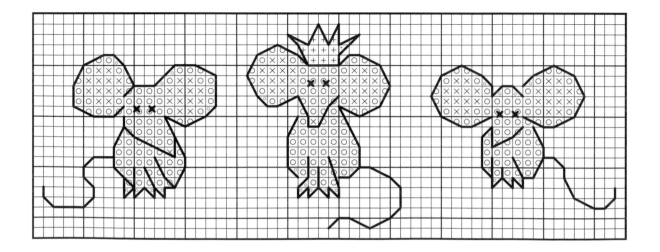

	KEY for the Trio from Oz		
	DMC	Colour	Stitches
U	301	red-brown	190
▲	350	red	19
●	413	charcoal	11
S	437	light brown	42
−	472	green	102
T	646	dark grey	26
X	809	blue	263
<	972	gold	420
N	976	brown	25
·	3072	silver-grey	459
O	3747	pale blue	169
+		white	6
	413	charcoal	backstitch

Placemat

The design shown on the previous page features Dorothy and her faithful companion Toto on the yellow brick road; it would make a lovely mat for a child's dressing table.

Materials: 24 x 24 cm pale yellow linen with 28 threads per inch; DMC embroidery threads listed.

Stitch count: 76H x 80W

Directions: Stitch the design in the centre of the fabric and press the work carefully when complete.

Machine a line of staystitching approximately 13 mm in from each edge. Remove the threads outside the staystitching to form a fringe all around the mat. The mat can be handwashed every now and then.

	KEY for Dorothy & Toto		
	DMC	Colour	Stitches
L	301	red-brown	99
▼	350	red	89
■	413	charcoal	2
Z	414	grey	209
T	702	dark green	205
X	704	green	470
U	726	yellow	1065
↑	754	peach	151
N	798	dark blue	40
O	809	blue	211
*	976	brown	324
–	3747	pale blue	549
+		white	285
•	5283	metallic silver	89
	413	charcoal	backstitch

Where's Wally?

The elusive Wally is the creation of Martin Handford who, as a child, liked nothing better than to draw huge battle scenes. When he grew up and became a freelance illustrator he special-ised in drawing crowd scenes. So it was perhaps inevitable that when he created his first book, it would be Where's Wally?, a collection of scenes so jam-packed with detail and amusing goings-on that it would keep children absorbed for hours. It was so successful that Martin followed it up with other titles, in which Wally traipses through Hollywood, travels to fantastic lands or trips through world history. Each double-page spread takes eight weeks to draw and, amongst all the mayhem, you might succeed in finding Wally, his friends Wenda, Woof the dog, Whitebeard the wizard and naughty Odlaw. With over thirty-six million copies sold, in more than twenty countries and nineteen languages, Wally has been just about everywhere!

Bookmark

Wally is a keen bookworm and a bookmark featuring him will prevent any child from losing their place. The picture is on page 102.

Materials: 20 x 10 cm white Aida fabric
with 16 thread groups per inch;
self-adhesive felt;
DMC embroidery threads listed.

Stitch count: 79H x 36W

Directions: Stitch the design, forming the eyes with french knots. Cross-stitch a border leaving thirteen squares above and below the design and three squares either side of the design. Trim the sides of the Aida just one square out from the border. Carefully pull out the excess horizontal threads to form a fringe top and bottom.

Cut the felt to fit the Aida fabric. Peel off the backing and stick the felt onto the wrong side of the stitching. If self-adhesive felt is not available, glue on ordinary felt with fabric glue.

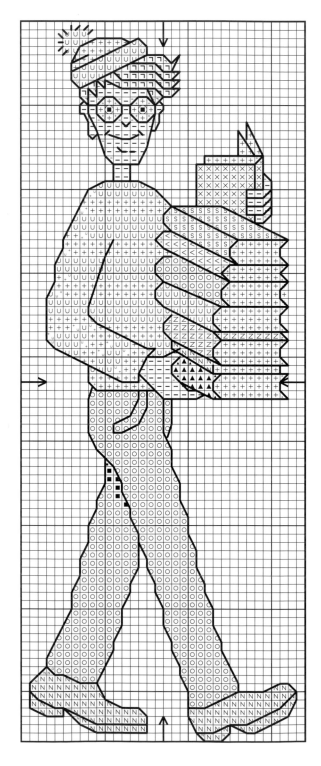

KEY for Wally reading		
DMC	Colour	Stitches
■ 310	black	2
⌐ 433	dark brown	37
N 435	brown	125
S 444	yellow	49
Z 553	purple	30
U 666	red	219
▲ 704	green	18
X 722	orange	40
< 893	pink	21
O 996	blue	434
− 3774	peach	98
+	white	330
310	black	backstitch

Badge

With a badge like the one shown overleaf, Wally-watchers will never be alone! It's a little fiddly, so you might like to stitch it on a larger fabric count.

Materials: 15 x 10 cm white Aida fabric with 18 thread groups per inch; white cardboard; a marking pen; a large safety pin; tape and PVA glue; DMC embroidery threads listed.

Stitch count: 70H x 31W

Directions: Stitch the design on the Aida and, when complete, lay it on a sheet of plastic. Mix PVA glue with water and gently brush it over the embroidery. Let it dry: the fabric should stiffen. Repeat if necessary.

Trim the fabric, leaving one unstitched row all round the design. Cut a piece of stiff white cardboard slightly larger than the trimmed fabric. Run around the edges with a blue highlighter. Glue the embroidery onto the cardboard.

Tape a large safety pin onto the back of the badge so it can be pinned onto clothing.

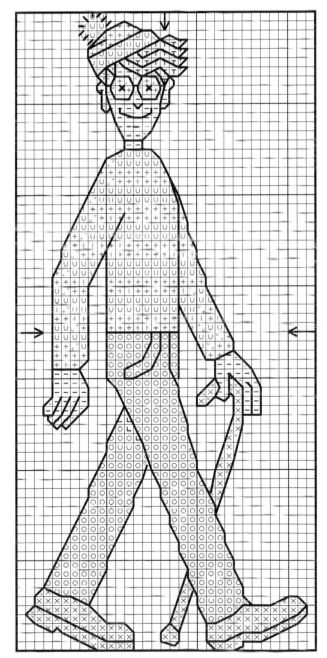

KEY for Wally hiking			
	DMC	Colour	Stitches
■	310	black	2
L	317	dark grey	9
T	433	dark brown	38
X	435	brown	185
U	666	red	250
O	996	blue	411
−	3774	peach	132
+		white	238
	310	black	backstitch

Wally-watchers everywhere can delight their friends with this clever pocket. The chart is on page 108.

Fans will always know where Wally is when they're wearing this badge. Instructions appear on page 105.

Secret Pocket

This pocket, pictured on page 107, opens to reveal something most surprising: Wally!

Materials: 35 x 15 cm white Aida fabric
            with 16 thread groups per inch;
            white backing fabric;
            red cotton fabric;
            a button; cord;
            DMC embroidery threads listed.

Stitch count: 45H x 65W

Directions: Orient the Aida so that the
15 cm edges are top and bottom. Stitch the
design, starting 2 cm below the top edge.
Back with a piece of white fabric. From each
top corner, mark a point 2 cm in and another 6 cm down. Baste 1 cm in from edges,
using the marks as guides for the flap shape.

Cut red fabric to match and 10 cm cord.
Assemble: red fabric, cord looped at the top
with ends aligned to the fabric edge, and
embroidery face down. Sew the sides and
flap edge along basting. Trim flap corners
and turn right side out. Turn and handsew
the raw edges. (If you wish to sew the pocket
onto a garment, do so before the next step.)
Fold the pocket section up by 12.5 cm and
handsew the sides. Sew a button in place.

	KEY for Wally waving		
	DMC	Colour	Stitches
■	310	black	2
−	414	dark grey	5
+	433	dark brown	210
O	666	red	274
U	3774	peach	768
✕		white	302
	310	black	backstitch

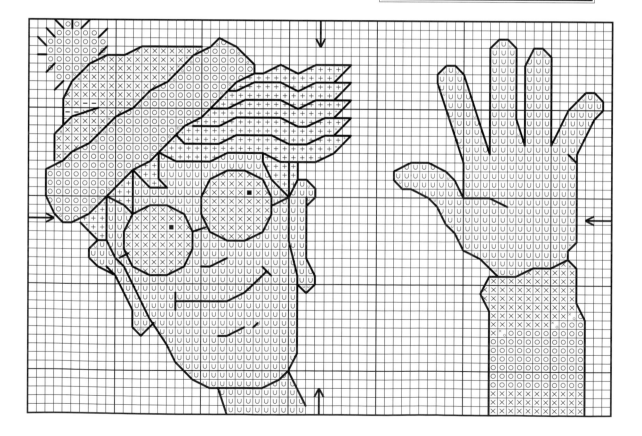

Wally Game

The special Where's Wally? game shown overleaf takes a while to make but will be worth every moment. The movable faces can also be used as badges!

Materials: 43 x 70 cm white Aida fabric with 14 thread groups per inch; blue cotton fabric; white cardboard; Velcro tape; five buttons; thin dowel; tape; wide and narrow ribbon; DMC embroidery threads listed.

Stitch count: 50H x 40W (each face)

Directions: Cut five 14 cm squares of Aida and stitch a face on each one. Cut five 10 cm squares of cardboard. Cover each cardboard square with a face, taping edges neatly on the back. Stitch a hooked section of Velcro tape on the back of each face.

Make the flaps as follows. Cut five 13.5 x 28.5 cm pieces of Aida. On each of these, stitch a question mark starting 45 mm from the right edge. Cut five 13.5 x 28.5 cm pieces of blue fabric. Lay the Aida and the blue fabric pieces in pairs, right sides together. Cut a strip of paper 11.5 x 26.5 cm and shape one end like the flap of an envelope. Use this paper template to mark a stitching line on the back of each Aida strip. Machine sew the pieces together, leaving a gap at the unshaped narrow end. Trim the corners and turn the flap right side out. Cut five 8 cm pieces of narrow ribbon. Handsew the opening closed, fixing a loop of ribbon in place as you do so. Sew a furry

section of Velcro tape on the inside right half of each flap. Fold the flap over, position a button and sew it in place.

Make the backing section as follows. Cut a 104 x 47 cm piece of blue fabric and fold it lengthwise, right sides facing. Sew 1 cm seams up either side to form a bag. Turn it right side out and turn in the raw edges of the opening. Cut five 12 cm pieces of wide ribbon and arrange them as hanging loops in the opening. Machine sew the opening closed, securing the ribbon loops. Position the five flaps on the backing and machine sew a 9 cm square around the Velcro to secure. Stick a face inside each flap.

Cut 44 cm thin dowel and paint it blue. Insert this through the hanging loops. To play the game, rearrange the faces and ask children to guess where Wally is hiding.

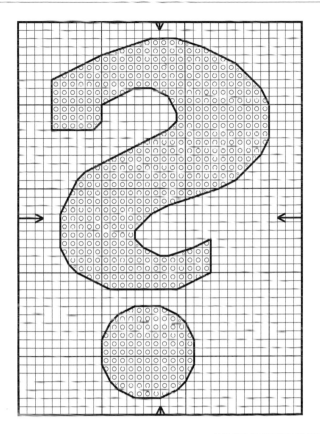

KEY for Wally and Friends

	DMC	Colour	Stitches
■	310	black	152
✳	414	dark grey	235
−	415	grey	62
⌐	433	dark brown	511
∪	444	yellow	291
○	666	red	1739
<	945	apricot	1012
✕	996	blue	416
+		white	1838
	310	black	backstitch

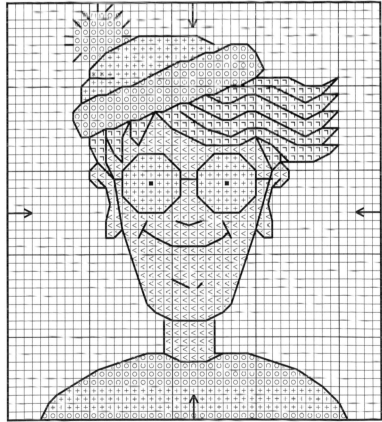

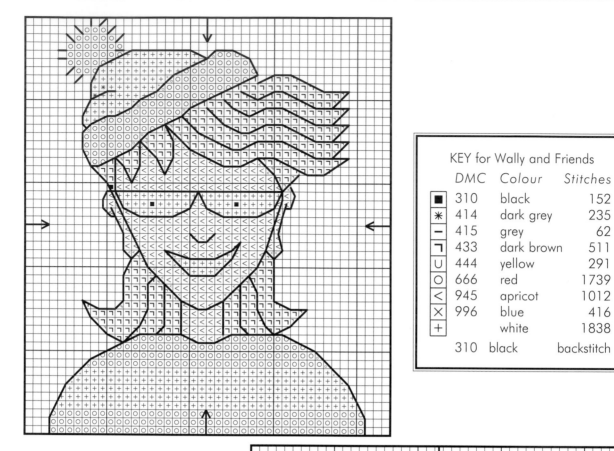

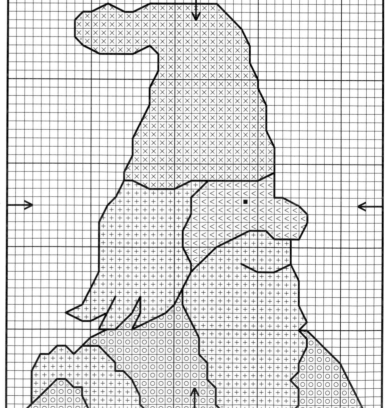

Where's Wally? © Martin Handford 2000

The Little Prince

As the Second World War raged, a French air pilot living in exile in New York penned a tale which summed up the fragile state of the world. The Little Prince, *perfectly written and illustrated by Antoine de Saint-Exupéry, is a story for children and adults alike. The narrator is, like the author, a pilot who has been stranded in the Sahara Desert. Here he befriends the Little Prince who tells of life on his own small planet and of his care for a beautiful but haughty flower; the result is a powerful fable about the nature of love. The wise-but-innocent Little Prince continues to win the hearts of all those who read his story and he is revered by generations everywhere. In his native France, he has even featured on a banknote!*

114

Height Chart

Measure your child's growth with this charming height chart pictured on page 115.

Materials: 90 x 22 cm cream Aida fabric with 11 threads groups per inch; white lining fabric; ribbon; thin dowel; DMC embroidery threads listed.

Stitch count: 75H x 73W (picture only)

Directions: Stitch the design at the top of the Aida fabric, allowing 4 cm above. Cross-stitch '120' (the top height mark) 3 cm below the design at the left-hand side and backstitch a line across the chart (see page 124 for the numbers). Cross-stitch '115' 5 cm below, at the right hand side, and add a backstitch line. Continue on down the chart, stitching each number 5 cm below the previous one, ending on '60 cm'. (The chart must be hung the correct height above floor level.)

    Zigzag the edges of the Aida fabric and carefully press the work. Cut a matching piece of white lining fabric and sew it and the Aida together, right sides facing, along each long side, 5 mm from the edge. Turn right side out. Topstitch along each edge.

    Cut six 8 cm lengths of ribbon and fold each one in half. Pin three ribbon loops in the top opening and three in the bottom. Handsew the openings closed, securing the ribbon loops. Cut two 20 cm lengths of thin dowel and insert them through the loops.

	DMC	Colour	Stitches
T	340	purple	39
U	341	pale purple	209
N	743	gold	151
O	996	blue	631
+	3607	pink	589
<	3743	pale mauve	40
X	3774	peach	120
•		white	148
	535	dark grey	backstitch

KEY for the Little Prince

To adults, Drawing Number One is obviously a hat. To the Little Prince (and others with understanding) it's clearly a boa constrictor which has swallowed an elephant.

He sees a bonfire smoking
Pigeons in the sky
His mother cleaning windows
A dog going by.

He sees his sisters searching
For a jar or tin
To take up to the park
And catch fishes in.

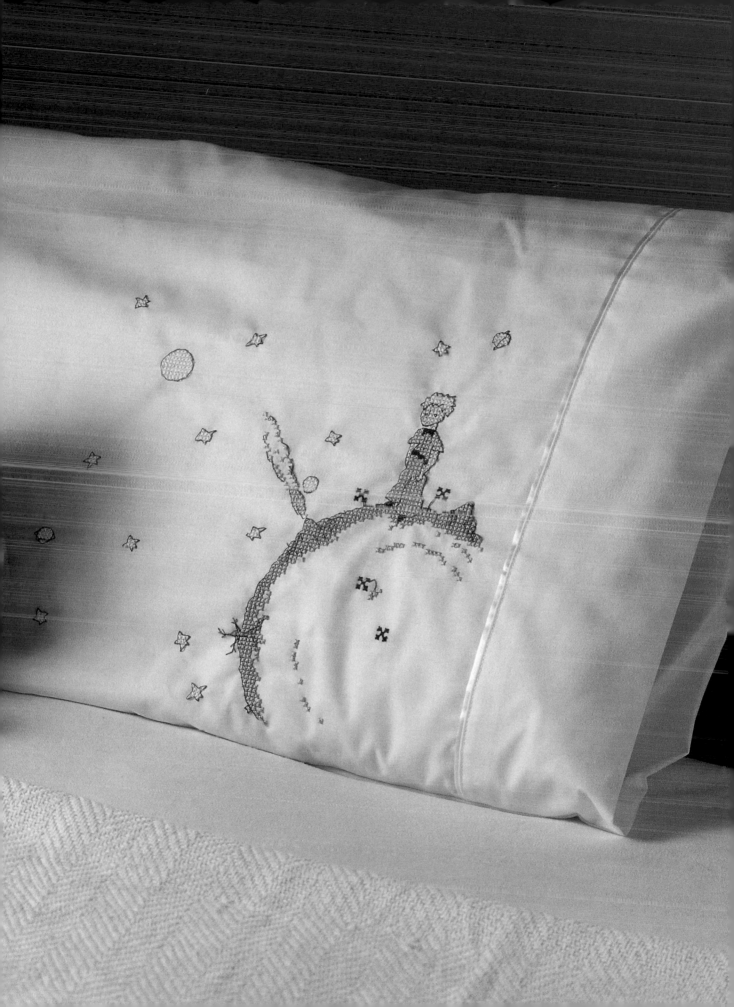

Pillowcase

This charming design features the Little Prince on Asteroid B-612. It has been stitched over waste canvas onto a pillowcase and is pictured on pages 118-9.

Materials: 28 x 30 cm waste canvas
with 11 thread groups per inch;
a white cotton pillowcase;
DMC embroidery threads listed.

Stitch count: 110H x 118W

Directions: Position the waste canvas at the bottom right of the pillowcase, near the opening. Tack around the edges and also diagonally so that the canvas is securely attached to one layer of the pillowcase.

Stitch the design, then remove the tacking threads. Dampen the canvas with a cloth and carefully remove the strands of the waste canvas, one by one.

Note: You could save waste canvas by using small scraps to stitch outlying planets.

	KEY for Asteroid B-612		
	DMC	Colour	Stitches
N	307	yellow	232
U	564	green	141
⌐	606	red	30
<	775	pale blue	36
X	948	peach	57
O	3042	mauve	48
T	3740	dark purple	6
–	3743	pale mauve	400
	535	dark grey	backstitch

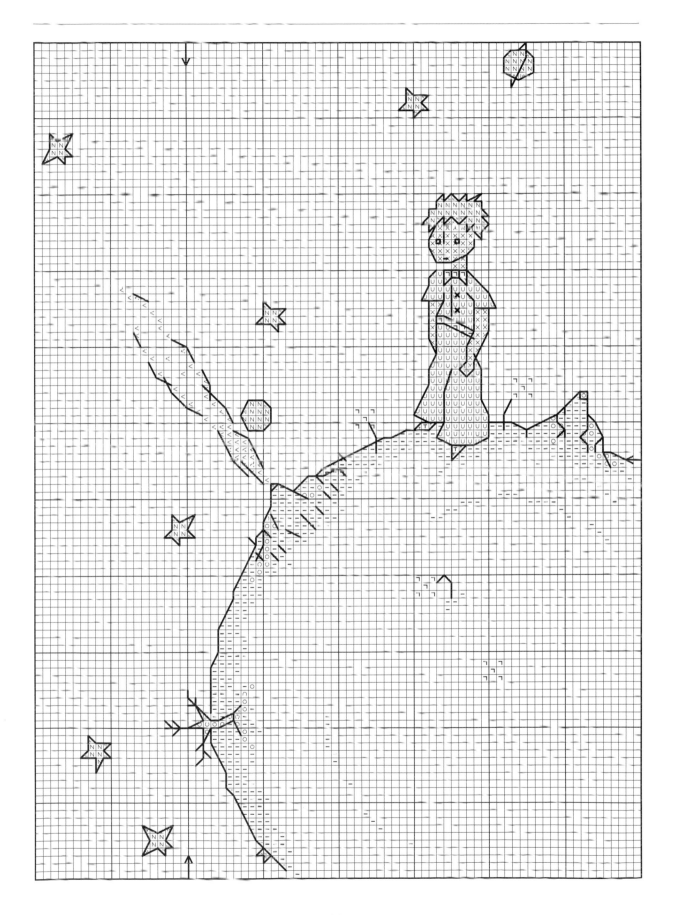

Designs for Kids

Here are some simple motifs for children who
want to learn to cross-stitch. Use chart colours
as a guide for suitable thread colours.

These alphabets and numbers can be used to add a child's name to many projects.

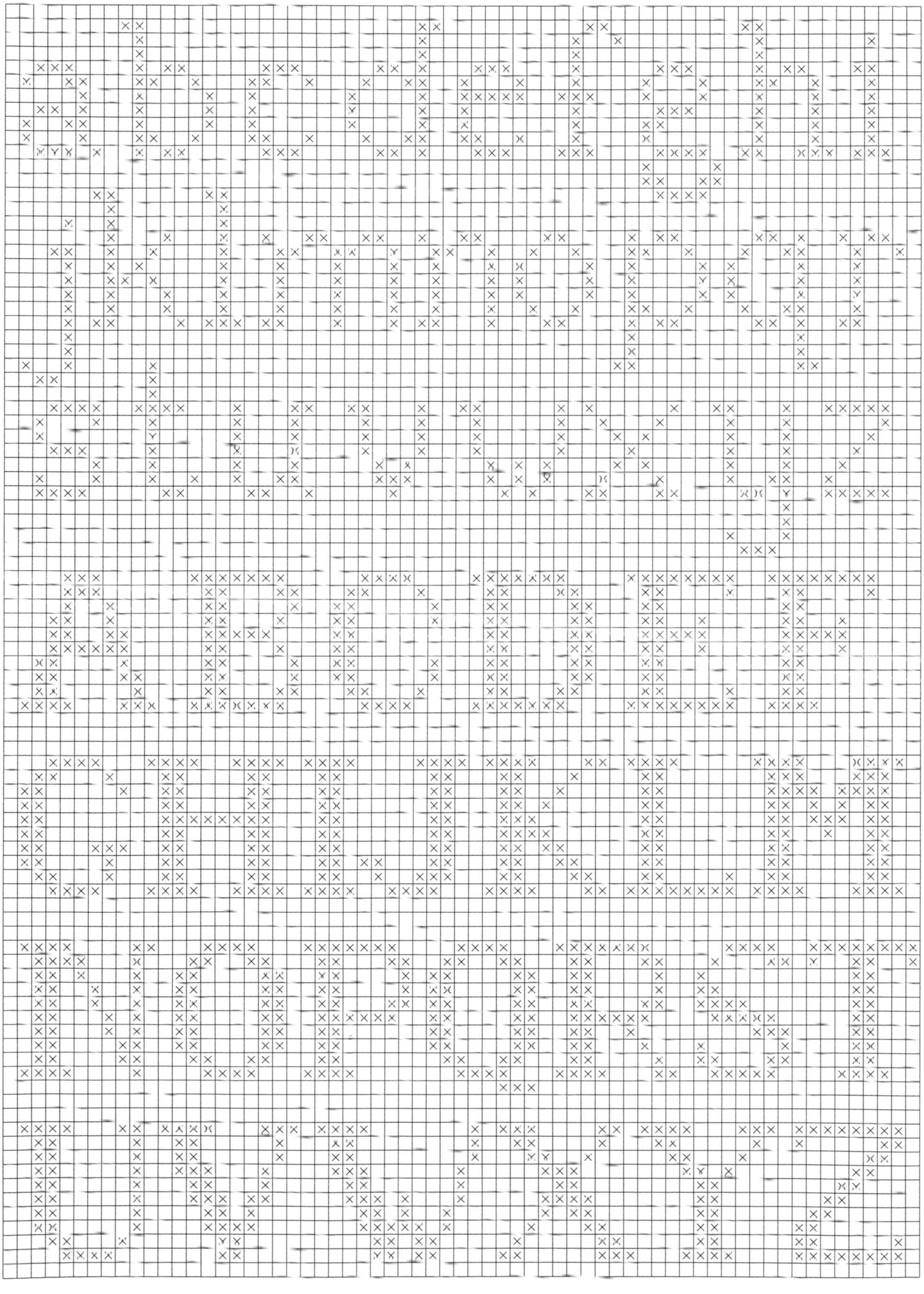

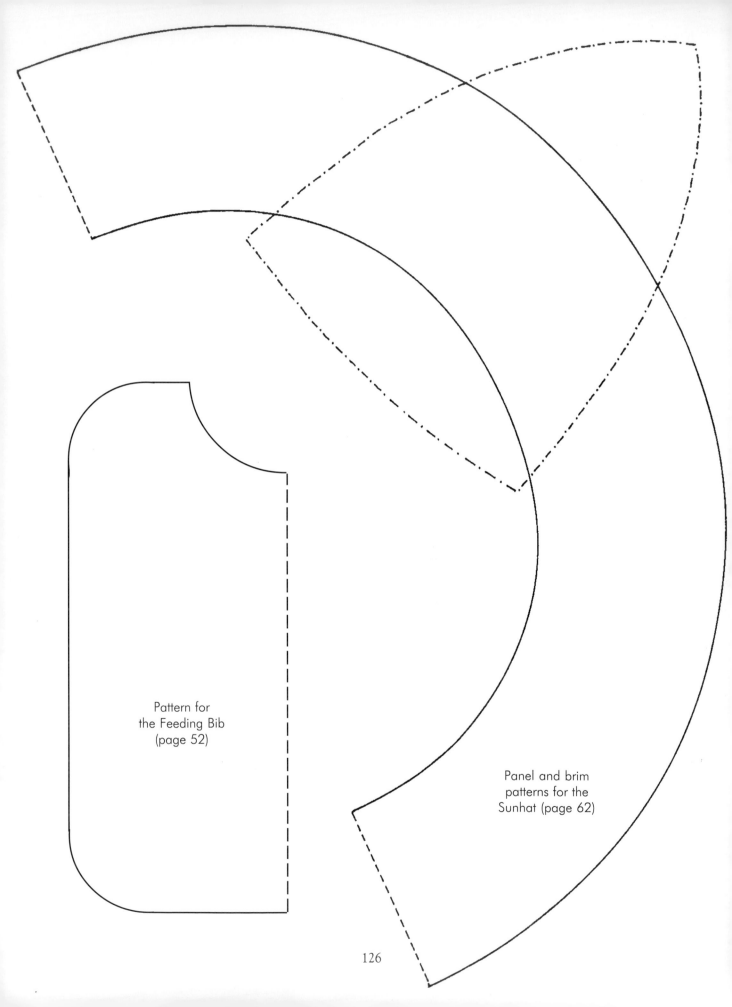

Pattern for
the Feeding Bib
(page 52)

Panel and brim
patterns for the
Sunhat (page 62)

126

Acknowledgements

The charts in this book were created with StitchCraft, a Windows-based software program
for designing counted charts. For information on this program, please contact:
Crafted Software at PO Box 78, Wentworth Falls NSW 2782 Australia,
Telephone: +61 2 4757 3136 Fax: +61 2 4757 3337   E-mail: stitch@pnc.com.au
Internet site: http://www.pnc.com.au/~stitch

Thanks to Mary Kuitert and Suzanne Masters for assistance with stitching.

Index